Tarot Ultimate Guide

The Supreme Guide for Learning the Art of Tarot Divination and Readings

Serra Night

Table of Contents

Introduction 4

Chapter 1: The History of Tarot 6
    The Meaning of Tarot Cards 8

Chapter 2: Tarot and Archetypes 12
    Jungian Archetypes Found in the Tarot 15
    Common Archetypes in the Tarot 17

Chapter 3: The Major Arcana 22
    0 – The Fool 23
    1 – The Magician 25
    2 – The High Priestess 27
    3 – The Empress 29
    4 – The Emperor 31
    5 – The Hierophant 33
    6 – The Lovers 35
    7 – The Chariot 37
    8 – Strength 39
    9 – The Hermit 41
    10 – The Wheel of Fortune 43
    11 – Justice 45
    12 – The Hanged Man 48
    13 – Death 50
    14 – Temperance 53
    15 – The Devil 55
    16 – The Tower 57
    17 – The Star 60
    18 – The Moon 62
    19 – The Sun 64
    20 – Judgment 67
    21 – The World 70

Chapter 4: Tarot and the Unconscious 73

Chapter 5: Tarot and Numerology 77
   Minor Arcana 78
   Major Arcana 83
   Master Numbers in Numerology 85

Chapter 6: Tarot and the Zodiac **88**
   The Suits and Their Corresponding Signs 89
   Court Cards 92
   Cardinal, Fixed, and Mutable Signs 94

Chapter 7: Tarot and the Chakras 97
   The Importance of Balance of the Chakras 98
   Why You Need to Read Your Tarot Cards 102
   The Chakras and the Tarot 103

Chapter 8: Tarot and Religion 107

Conclusion 110

Introduction

Thank you for your interest in this book. If you are reading this, it is because you are keen on learning more about the Tarot and how this ancient form of divination can be used to gain a deeper perspective on yourself and others around you.
Tarot is an age-old means of learning about the hidden aspects of our lives. It can be used to unveil traits that we might not necessarily be aware of. In addition, it can help us to become consciously aware of the things that make us tick. Indeed, the Tarot in a way in which you can really go down the path of self-discovery.

Yet, the Tarot is often dismissed as quackery as a result of its widespread use by fortune tellers and so-called psychics. There abound self-proclaimed experts who allude to the use of the Tarot as a means of predicting the future. These individuals are commonly found everywhere. Consequently, their inappropriate use of the Tarot has led a vast majority of people to become skeptical about its actual purpose of usefulness.
In this book, you will learn about what the Tarot actually is and what it can be used for. While there is no denying that it is a powerful tool that can be used to reveal general trends transiting from the present to the future, it should be noted that this book is not about learning how to predict the future. Rather, this book is about learning what the Tarot is about and how you can use it to learn more about yourself and others around you.

Furthermore, this book will help you get a handle on what the individual cards represent and the common archetypes that they are based on. As you will see, each card has a reason for being; they are not merely nice-looking pictures that you can use to "tell the future." Each card speaks to one, or more, aspects of your personality. As such, the meanings attached to each card will help you to hone your senses.

That being said, anyone who is interested in this topic stands to gain from this book. So, whether you are a novice or a seasoned veteran in the Tarot, you will find something useful. You will surely find something that can stimulate your curiosity and take you from a passing curiosity to a serious pursuit of further knowledge. Best of all, you don't actually need to be versed in the Tarot to take advantage of this book. Everything you need to know to get started is right here.

We know that there is a great deal of information out there. Unfortunately, it is scattered all over the internet. In addition, print books are not easy to find on this subject. This is why we have incorporated everything you need to know into a single volume. That way, you won't have to go scouring all over the internet, or local bookstores for that matter, in order to find all of the information you have been looking for.

So, do take the time to go over every one of the topics in this book. You will find that they are all interconnected. Thus, it is highly recommended that you read this book in the sequence that it is presented. In this manner, you will be able to fully comprehend the information that we have presented herein.

Moreover, the information contained in this book may lead you down the path to other pursuits. So, we recommend that you keep this volume handy for easy reference down the road. That way, you can always refer back to it any time that you need to do so. Thank you once again for taking the time to read this book. Great care was taken in putting it together. We hope that you will find it both interesting and informative. Now, let's get on with it!

Chapter 1: The History of Tarot

Playing cards are very old and first showed up in Europe sometime around the late 1300s. Playing cards are thought to have been brought to Europe from Egypt and had four suits: batons (or polo sticks), coins (sometimes referred to as disks), swords, and cups. These four suits are very similar to the four suits in modern playing card decks, including tarot, and were the original inspiration for the four common suits that we still use today. Tarot cards have been around for centuries; however, with the oldest known playing card deck that resembled the modern tarot deck was made sometime between the years 1418 and 1425. This was a 60-card deck with 16 cards that featured images of several Greek gods and with four suits, each depicting a different kind of bird. This commissioned deck of playing cards, and others like it, would go on to inspire the first legitimate tarot packs, which were recorded to have been made in the 1440s in Bologna, Ferrara, Florence, and Milan. These decks added trump cards to the typical four suits that many decks contained. These new decks were referred to as "carte da trionfi," with the additional trump cards being called simply as "trionfi," which was later translated to trumps in English. The earliest documented mention of the trionfi was in a written statement in the Florence court records from the year 1440, referring to the transfer of two separate decks to Sigismondo Pandolfo Malatesta at that time. The oldest tarot cards that still survive today are about 15 of the Visconti-Sforza decks, which were painted sometime around the middle of the 15th century. There was also an expanded tarot deck that was commonly used in Florence, which featured 97 separate cards and included things like the four classical elements, astrological symbols, and many of the traditional tarot motifs of that period.

Tarot cards can seem confusing at times, with their ancient iconography and their use of religious imagery, historical events, and various ancient symbols. To those who are not familiar with the cards and their symbolism, they might even seem evil or unholy. A Dominican preacher even talked about the inherent evil of the tarot cards in a sermon during the 15th century, referencing their use in gambling and divinatory practices and spoke out against the use of the tarot. The main use of these cards was entertainment, but some people chose to use them for things like fortune-telling, as well. This is the source of a lot of misconceptions of the nature of the kind of "divination" that is performed with the use of tarot cards, which causes a lot of people to dismiss them as frivolous and foolish; some people even condemned them as "evil." To outsiders and skeptics who dismiss the existence of the "magic" that they believe tarot divination to utilize, the use of these cards can seem silly or pointless. However, the "magic" of the kind of divination that can be performed with the use of tarot cards doesn't come from some mystical force. If you take a closer look at the tarot deck, and the meanings of each card, then the true nature of the tarot will become much clearer. Each card represents a different stage of human emotional and mental development and a different aspect of human life. The small, static images that are depicted on each of the tarot cards can be used to reveal many of the most common and complicated struggles or desires that human beings experience and can help us understand our circumstances in order to better understand or shape the outcome of certain events that are happening in our lives or will happen soon. The "magic" of tarot decks comes from simple psychological practices, rather than a mystical force manipulating your fate to show you the cards that you need.

The Meaning of Tarot Cards

The specific meanings of different cards have changed over the years, as well. Divination cards have been altered and changed to reflect the culture of the current era and the needs of their users. This is a large part of why these cards can be so difficult for "outsiders" to understand. Many different tarot decks, especially some of the older ones, contain references or allegories to specific people or events that occurred in the past, sometimes even many centuries earlier. Before the 18th century, a lot of the imagery that exists on the cards of the tarot deck applied to a much larger audience much more directly because they were designed for the people of that time. However, there have been several shifts in the attitudes and mentalities that people carry since then, and as a result, some people find it much more difficult to understand and relate to the meanings on most tarot decks today. Many of the modern tarot cards are either very simple or extremely confusing, still using a number of signs and symbols that most people simply do not recognize immediately unless they have already done some research on the meanings of the cards.

The use of cards for the purposes of this kind of divination goes back to around the 4th century, and many people believe that this practice originated with the cards for a game that was played in Turkey called Mamluk. Sometime around the 1500s, a group of Italian aristocrats had discovered a game called "Tarocchi Appropriati," which had players dealing random cards and using common thematic associations in the meanings of the cards to write simple poetic verses about themselves and the other players, similar to the more modern game "MASH." Even the earliest tarot decks were designed for games, like the "carte da trionfi" decks that were commissioned by a number of wealthy Italian families to be used in a game that was similar to Bridge. The cards in these decks contained the four suits that we still use today—cups, coins, swords, and sticks (which would later become wands)—as well as face cards, including the king and two male underlings. Tarot cards would later be developed to include a queen, the "trump" cards, and a "fool" card for a total of 78 cards in a single deck.

The artwork that was displayed on the tarot cards' faces was meant to reflect various aspects of the real world that the players of these games lived in at the time. Some people believed that this imagery was also intended to create a realistic narrative within the play of the game that they were created for, which makes sense if you consider the nature of many of the games that have been played with tarot cards throughout the years. This also allows the cards to reflect common archetypes and experiences in a typical human life and led to the use of tarot cards for divination later on as people began to play these games on their own, or even applied the games that they played with the cards and the narratives that they created and likely related to themselves or the people they played with.

One of the most common tarot decks today is the "Rider-Waite" deck, which has been the most popular version of the tarot deck since the early 1900s. This deck is named after its own publisher William Rider and a popular mystic named A.E. Waite, who had the deck illustrated. The Rider-Waite deck is responsible for bringing the tarot to popularity with modern mystical readers and for divinatory readings. This deck was originally designed to be used for divination, and many decks included a book written by Waite, which described and explained a lot of the meanings behind all of the imagery and symbolism that the cards contained.

The tarot is definitely one of the most widely known kinds of card decks used for divinatory purposes, but there are other kinds that exist as well. Some of these are the common 52 playing card deck that you will see more commonly or any of the common "oracle decks" that can be purchased outside of the typical tarot, like the Lenormand deck. An interesting fact to note about the tarot, however, is that the original tarot decks that came from Egypt were said to have had a number of Egyptian symbols in their illustrations, which helped in the popularization of this deck over a number of the other kinds of oracle decks. Although the Egyptian system of hieroglyphs had not been deciphered by that point, as the rosetta stone would not be discovered until the year 1799, a large portion of European people in the 18th century thought it was possible that the Egyptian people had a deep insight about the nature of human existence. When the tarot cards were revealed to have a number of Egyptian symbols on their illustrations, a lot of people connected the new tarot cards to the perceived insights of the Egyptian people and began to flock to the tarot over many of the other oracle card decks for the purposes of divination. Additionally, it was also said that the tarot deck was based on the Book of Thoth and was made by Thoth's priests into several gold plates, which served as inspiration for the original tarot decks. They were eventually redesigned as the first card deck that was intended explicitly for divination and cartomancy.

Chapter 2: Tarot and Archetypes

An important thing to learn about tarot is the concept of the Jungian archetypes. Carl Jung is considered to have been one of the founders of analytical psychology, and while he never directly mentioned tarot cards specifically in any of his work, there are very clear connections to the concepts that he helped develop and the concepts and ideas behind the tarot. One of Jung's most influential contributions to the theory of psyche was the introduction of archetypal images and the idea of the collective unconscious, which are significant concepts of the tarot. The concept of the collective unconscious was largely developed and popularized by Jung, who believed that every individual possesses their own personal "conscious" mind, which contains all of the knowledge and all of the memories that a person has experienced in his or her life up to a particular point in time. This is the active mind, and what most people commonly think of as the "self." All of the memories and knowledge that you actively draw upon rests within this personal conscious mind. There is also a "personal unconscious" below the personal conscious. The personal unconscious is very similar to the personal conscious; the main difference lies in the fact that it contains the memories and knowledge that a person has forgotten or repressed but have still been experienced in the past. These memories still belong to you and you alone, whether you actively remember it or not. The memories and experiences within the personal unconscious are "hidden away" from the person and were "locked away" or otherwise lost for some reason or another, whether they were traumatic memories or simply unimportant ones that the person did not need. However, while these memories and experiences cannot be recalled, they can still impact the person whom they belong to, in the form of "unexplained" habits or caution that the person takes without an apparent reason for doing so. These repressed or "lost" memories can be revealed or uncovered through therapy, hypnosis, or meditation for a number of reasons, but as they stand in the personal unconscious, the person will not be actively aware of those memories.

Tarot cards can also sometimes reveal the concepts of these unconscious memories or experiences through their imagery. There is another state that people possess that exists outside of the personal conscious and unconscious, which is called the "superconscious." The superconscious is where our "higher self" exists, as well as the experiences and memories from our "past lives" and the things that we learned during those lives. Tarot relates to this concept by using the superconscious and the ways that it will affect the personal unconscious to reveal things about ourselves that we may not have realized or fully understood. The superconscious is also thought to be our primary source of connection to the divine and other universal forces. One of the most common and simplest tarot spreads uses three cards to tell us about our past, present, and future. The idea behind this spread is that we will arrange our tarot deck and choose our cards based on the experiences that we have had that have been hidden within our unconscious mind through the superconscious. Carl Jung believed that we could "tell the future" by examining and evaluating our past and the ways that our past choices have affected the events that followed them, as well as our present situations. This is similar to the concept behind a very famous aphorism, which was even adopted by Winston Churchill, "Those who fail to learn from history are condemned to repeat it."

Jungian Archetypes Found in the Tarot

Jung also believed that there was another realm beyond the personal mind, an unconscious mind that every person contributes to and draws from. Jung believed that if you stepped below the personal unconscious, you would find a deeper level, which was called the "collective unconscious." The collective unconscious contained all the general experiences that all of mankind shared since their creation, as well as all the records of mankind's evolution over the years. The memories and experience that were contained within the collective unconscious are owned collectively by every person in the world.

Every person in the world also has access to the collective unconscious and can draw from it for inspiration or information relating to the common experiences that all or most human people encounter. The collective unconscious is not made up of specific memories or experiences but of common symbols and archetypes. A lot of people believe that the collective unconscious is accessed by people in the form of our dreams. The archetypes, or the models which we use to identify general concepts and ideas, are common or regular patterns of behavior that can be noticed in different kinds of people from different backgrounds or in different situations that we might encounter. There is an archetype, usually multiple archetypes that can be applied to any person or situation that we might encounter in our lives. As humans continue to grow and develop, we find new archetypes to add to the list as we encounter new things or unexpected situations that we cannot explain with ones that already exist. These archetypes can be thought of in a similar way to the tropes that we used to describe film or television characters or stories. As we create new television shows or movies, they will change our perception of existing tropes, and if we encounter a new kind of character or story, we will add it to our list of different kinds of tropes. Similarly, examples of different archetypal concepts can be found in everything and everyone that we come across throughout our lives.

The symbols and archetypes that we use to describe different situations and entities all reside within what we refer to as the collective unconscious. One good example of a common archetype is the "mother" figure from just about every culture around the world. Every person who has ever existed has had a figure that acted as a mother to them or is familiar with the idea of a mother figure. Of course, every person has to be born from their mother, so it would make sense that most cultures share the same or similar ideas of what a mother is. These are figures like Mary or Gaia or any number of deities and characters that act as a "mother" to humankind. This archetype might not manifest itself in the same specific ways for every individual person, but the basic concept of "the mother" is essentially the same, no matter what your personal experiences are. A mother figure is a person who is caring, loving, and nurturing and someone who sees to your physical and emotional growth and well-being.

The theory behind this concept is that all of most people have relatively consistent connections to these common archetypes and that these archetypal images form the foundation for our perception and affect the ways that we think about and perceive our experiences and tell stories about our lives.

Common Archetypes in the Tarot

Some common archetypes that can be seen in almost every culture are the "anima" and the "animus." These represent two parts of a union that makes up the whole and complete "self." These concepts represent the masculine and feminine parts that every person possesses. These concepts of the masculine and feminine aspects of people and the world exist in most cultures, and an important part of being a well-balanced and mentally healthy person is the ability to understand and accept both the masculine and feminine aspects of yourself and the world. It is also important to understand that while the anima and animus describe traits that are commonly viewed as "masculine" and "feminine," these traits exist in every person regardless of their sex or gender. Every person has aspects and qualities that relate to both the anima and the animus, and whatever way you choose to identify with any of these qualities is absolutely fine. For tarot cards, this means that cards that represent feminine figures can still apply to a man and vice versa. These cards simply use imagery that is easy for us to understand and relate to the archetypes that we probably already know; the masculine and feminine animus and anima are figures that we are familiar with and can help provide us with insight about ourselves with common archetypal symbols.

The lovers are a good representation of the concepts of anima and animus, as they represent a union of masculine and feminine figures. The characters represented on these cards are also typically depicted as having opposing or conflicting natures. Another good card that represents the concepts of the anima and the animus is the world card. This is a card similar to the lovers, but it deals with a larger scale, representing the union of all the different parts of the world.

There are also other important aspects of ourselves that will be important to keep in mind. One is the persona. Carl Jung described the persona as the "masks" that different people show to the world and the people around them. These personas manifest as the ways that we present ourselves and how we would like to be perceived within our societies. These are common archetypes that people will portray to the people around them, like the artist, the scholar, or the leader. Jung also believed that a healthy person would be able to maintain multiple personas and could be much more flexible with the personas that they could align themselves with. It can even be argued that the ability to maintain and align yourself with multiple different personas, along with an understanding of them, is required in order to be mentally and emotionally healthy as a person.

The shadow is also another important concept to understand. Where personas are the parts of ourselves that we project to the people around us and to the world as a whole, the shadow represents the parts of ourselves that we reject. All the aspects of ourselves that we hide from the people around us, and, sometimes, from ourselves are all potential parts that make up our "shadows." For example, you might be kind of rude or malicious sometimes. Everyone can be, at times, but those qualities can be difficult to accept in ourselves. When you reject those qualities, they can become detached and almost like a separate part of ourselves that we try to push away or "brush under the carpet."

Shadows are the archetypal basis for a lot of the monsters and the concepts that make up our perception of "evil." A very important part of becoming a healthy and mature human being is being able to understand your "shadows" and accept them as parts of you, instead of simply rejecting them. One card that can be easily related to the concept of the shadow is "the devil." The devil is commonly used to represent the concept of the shadow. Things like addiction and detachment and the ability to come to terms with those qualities and explore them as a part of you are some of the basic concepts of the devil card. Death is also a good card that can be used to relate to the shadow. Death is something that most people fear. Death follows you from the womb throughout the course of your life and is an objective fact regardless of whether you acknowledge it or not. Coming to terms with the concept of death is an important part of developing as a person and will help to shape who you are and the way that you choose to live.

Another common archetype that is related to the concepts of the persona and the shadow is the "self." The concept of the self is a little bit more complicated, but the self can be thought of for the sake of simplicity as the unification of all of the archetypes and all of the different aspects of ourselves. Carl Jung believed that people are usually "whole" as children and become fragmented as they grow up and develop prejudices and insecurities, and the goal of our personal journey, once we reach adulthood, is to become whole again. This idea of the path to becoming whole and healthy can be seen clearly in the "first" (numbered 0) and last cards of the Tarot's major arcana, the fool, and the world. The fool most directly represents the concept of the "self." Each of the numbered major arcana cards represents a step along the "fool's journey" or the path that each person will walk toward becoming "whole." The last numbered major arcana card and the last step on the "fool's journey" is the world. The world represents the unification of all of the various aspects of the self in order to allow us (or the fool) to become whole again. The steps of the fool's journey, the cards that represent them, and their common archetypes are discussed in the following chapter.

Chapter 3: The Major Arcana

In this chapter, we are going to be looking at the Major Arcana in Tarot. Based on the Jungian archetypes discussed earlier, this set of cards represents the large, or major archetypes common to virtually all cultures throughout history.

0 – The Fool

The first of the cards that will be described here is the fool. The fool card most commonly depicts a young man who is carrying a small sack and walking carelessly ahead without paying attention to the dangers along his path. The fool walks forward, toward the edge of a cliff, about to take his final step off and fall off the edge. It is unclear whether he is unaware or if he simply does not care. There is also usually a dog following the fool, sometimes barking at him in an attempt to warn the fool about the dangers that he faces and the traps that he might fall into if he does not become aware of his surroundings. This gives the reader of this card the impression that if the fool does not realize the dangers ahead and act more cautiously, he might not be able to grow as a person and live out the adventures he dreams of. Some of the general concepts that the fool card represents are innocence, opportunities, and wonder. Because of these traits, a common archetype for this card is "the child."

All tarot cards have two meanings—one interpretation for the upright position and one for when the card is drawn upside-down. The fool also applies to this rule. Unlike most of the cards within the tarot deck's major arcana, as well as the minor arcana, the fool does not have a "real" number. The fool card holds the number 0, which is representative of the fool's potential for growth and development as he walks along the path called the fool's journey. Because of this potential and the number that represents it, the fool is also considered to be a blank slate, without a clear and developed personality. The fool is commonly seen as a symbol of innocence and as a representation of the "broken" state that people find themselves in and need to recover from in order to "build" themselves and become a whole and healthy person again.

Drawing the fool card, specifically in the upright position, typically represents opportunities. Things like new beginnings or the start of a journey, which will provide us with the opportunity to discover freedom from the typical constraints of mundane life. At the start of his journey, the fool sees each new day as its own adventure in a way that seems almost childish. He sees everything that happens to him as an opportunity and believes that anything is possible in the world. He leads a simple, carefree life and wishes to explore and develop the world, unburdened by any concern for what lies ahead, good or bad. The fool inspires courage among those around him, as he understands that each new day is an opportunity to discover new doors. Drawing the fool card is also sometimes interpreted as a "call to action," telling the recipient of this card that they should begin to embrace risks and new opportunities that present themselves. The fool carries the lesson in his mind that you can never know what lies ahead and that sometimes the only way to find out is to take a leap of faith. Good or bad, you will often find adventure.

However, when the fool is presented in the reversed or upside-down position, he shows some of his more "negative" or undesirable qualities to the recipient of this card. Presented in the reversed position, the fool card warns us to be cautious and careful and that they might even be acting "like a fool" by ignoring the consequences of our actions. Much like the careless figure that is depicted on this card, you might not be aware of a hazardous position that you are in or will find yourself soon unless you can learn to be more aware of your actions and your surroundings. The reversed fool card might be warning the recipient to take more care in planning for the future and being aware of the consequences of their actions, instead of simply "living in the moment." Much like the dog that is commonly depicted on this card, the reversed fool card warns the recipient against acting recklessly or allowing themselves to be taken advantage of. Some things are simply too good to be true, and the reversed fool card acts as a reminder of that fact.

1 – The Magician

The actual first numbered card of the major arcana is the magician. The magician card commonly depicts a figure with one hand pointing toward the heavens and one hand pointing to the ground. One common interpretation of the directions of the magician's hands is a connection to the phrase "as above, so below," which states that the earth reflects the heavens or that the "microcosm" is inspired by the "macrocosm." Another common interpretation is that the magician's hands are representative of his nature as a bridge between the heavens and the earth. The magician typically stands behind a table, which holds one item representative of each of the four symbols of the minor arcana's suits: swords, wands, pentacles, and cups, with an "infinity" symbol above his head, representing the infinite possibilities of creation with the will. For reasons that will most likely seem obvious, the magician is commonly connected to the concepts of power and magic, and a common archetype for the magician card is "the trickster."

When drawn upright, the magician represents the willpower of the recipient, as well as the concepts of creation, desire, and manifestation. With the power of the elements that he wields, the magician is capable of moving forward with the potential that is represented by the fool, molding himself and his desires in order to manifest them and realize his potential. The magician uses his willpower to realize his desires and acts as the link between the heavens and the earth by inciting change on earth to mirror the heavens. The upright magician tells his recipient to remember that they have the power to manifest their desires and realize their potential. Drawing the magician in the upright position can tell you that it might be time to stop hesitating and move forward in order to realize your full potential. This can relate to our lives in the forms of new opportunities, which we will need to take in order to grow and develop. Where the fool presents the possibility of new doors along our paths, the magician tells us that it's time to open those doors and begin to take action to mold our world into the one that we desire the most.

Drawing this card in the reversed position, however, represents a version of the magician who more closely embodies the "trickster" archetype. Where the upright magician represents action and power, the reversed magician is a being who is out of touch and uses trickery and illusions to get what he wants. The reversed magician is a warning to its recipient that they might need to make some changes in your life. This might take the form of a friend or another person in your life who pretends as if they have your interests in mind while simultaneously acting against you, or someone who will lure you in with their showmanship and charm in order to manipulate you for their personal gain. Drawing this card in the reversed position means that it might be time for you to evaluate yourself and the people around you. Maybe there is a person close to you who craves power and will manipulate you in order to achieve it, or it might even be possible that you have become obsessed with that power. In order to move forward and grow as a person, you will need to take care to avoid making careless choices that might lead to negative consequences for you and the people around you.

2 – The High Priestess

The second card representing a step along the fool's journey is the high priestess. The high priestess card commonly depicts a woman who sits with her hands in her lap on a cube-shaped stone placed between the pillars in Solomon's Temple—Boaz and Jachin. The pillar to the left of the empress, Jachin, is commonly seen as a symbol of establishment and order, whereas Boaz is representative of the concept of strength. A common interpretation of the meanings of these pillars is that they represent a number of different dual opposing concepts within nature, like the masculine and the feminine or good and evil. The high priestess and her position between these two pillars and on the porch of Solomon's Temple hint at her role as the mediator for fundamental opposing aspects of life and nature, even acting as the "third pillar." The high priestess understands the importance of opposing forces and represents the union of those forces. The high priestess is also very commonly shown with a crown, a cross, and a crescent moon at her feet. These items show her connection to the elements, nature, and emotional awareness. The high priestess is commonly connected to the concepts of intuition and emotion, and a common archetype for the magician card is "the Anima." When drawn upright, the high priestess represents the inner voice and intuition of the recipient, as well as the unconscious mind and inner knowledge. The magician card leans on the use of passion and desire to actively try to mold the world and manifest their desires. The high priestess suggests to her recipient that they should begin listening more closely to their intuition, as opposed to the conscious mind. The high priestess card most commonly depicts a dark, nighttime scene, representing a time when many people delve into introspection and self-growth. The high priestess instructs us to look within one's own self, instead of outward like the magician, for wisdom. The answers that you seek lie within your personal unconscious, and you will need to look there in order to move forward.

When the high priestess is drawn in the reversed position, she represents a lack or loss of center or your inner voice. You might be having trouble being able to find your center or to hear your inner voice. If this is the case, she advises you to meditate and look inside yourself for a new approach and ultimately trust in your intuition. Sometimes, your situation can be stressful, or you may find yourself being forced to make a difficult decision. Underestimating the value of looking within for the answers to our problems can lead us astray and cause us to "lose ourselves," acting discordantly. This can cause a sort of cognitive dissonance and is the cause of the kinds of actions and decisions that we come to regret with hindsight.

3 – The Empress

The third card representing a step along the fool's journey is the empress. The empress card commonly depicts a woman who sits on a throne in a field, surrounded by a large forest with a river flowing through it. The lush forest around the empress' throne represents her connection to nature and the earth and is commonly thought to represent the Earth Mother. The empress is also commonly associated with the concepts of fertility, harmony, and love. The empress has a crown of stars on her head, showing a deep connection with the divine. She is typically depicted wearing a robe patterned with pomegranates, which are representative of fertility and sits on cushions that show the symbol of Venus. The empress blesses the earth and the life within it with abundance and love. The empress is commonly connected to the concepts of nature, fertility, and motherhood, and a common archetype for the magician card is "the mother." The anima, which was mentioned earlier, is also a very good archetype for this card.

When drawn upright, the empress represents the feminine aspects of the recipient, as well as things like expression, creativity, and nurturing. The empress suggests to her recipient that they should begin to reach out and embrace an aspect of themselves that they might have neglected or might still be neglecting, leaning on the feminine aspects of themselves in order to foster growth and become a happier, well-adjusted person. The empress card pushes its recipient to begin to understand themselves on a deeper level and to appreciate and take care of yourself. Drawing the empress card upright might indicate motherhood or nurturing tendencies, possibly even pregnancy. She can also represent symbolic birth, such as a new idea or a new stage in your life, presenting you with opportunities for abundance and growth. Embrace these new opportunities and nurture them, and they are sure to bring you happiness and fortune.

When the empress is drawn in the reversed position, however, she acts as a warning to her recipient that they have begun to focus too heavily on other people or things and might be neglecting themselves as a result. While the empress is devoted to nurturing and caring for her loved ones, she can sometimes go too far and begin to overwhelm herself, or she might mean well in her actions to help the people around her but end up causing harm in the long run by solving everyone's problems for them. However, the empress simply represents an over-nurturing relationship. Being presented with the reversed empress card might not necessarily mean that you are too caring, or you would go too far trying to help others. You might find yourself on the other side of that coin, relying on other people to solve all of your problems for you or make decisions for you. If this is the case, the reversed empress pushes you to work toward finding your own action and being able to solve problems on your own.

4 – The Emperor

The fourth card representing a step along the fool's journey is the emperor. The emperor card commonly depicts a man in a position of power, most likely an emperor, sitting at his throne. This throne usually has four rams' heads on it at the top of the arm and the headrests, drawing a connection to his zodiac sign, Aries. In each hand, he typically holds a symbol of his power. His right hand holds a scepter, representing his power and right to rule as the emperor, and his left hand holds an orb, representing the lands that he keeps a watch over. The emperor is also most commonly shown to have a long beard, representing his age and experience, and the wisdom that comes with them. He is a just and old ruler, who learned over time how to rule his lands with power and authority, as well as the importance of order and how to maintain it for the sake of his people. While the empress leans on a kind and caring nature, the emperor relies on strength and power in order to maintain the order that he has worked so hard to achieve. The empress also represents the feminine, and the Emperor mirrors that by being a symbol of the masculine traits that exist within every person. The common concepts that the emperor is used to represent are authority, structure, order, control, and fatherhood. The most directly apparent archetype for this card is the animus, as it represents the masculine traits of human beings. Other common archetypes that are used to describe the emperor are the father and the hero.

When drawn upright, the emperor represents the masculine aspects of its recipient, as well as concepts such as authority, organization, structure, and fatherhood. The high priestess card leans on the use of intuition and introspection to allow herself to make the right decisions with confidence and without regret. The empress and the emperor balance the ideas of the high priestess by championing active choices and philosophies for the benefit of those around them. The emperor is a strategist, who lays plans before enforcing those plans until they have been completed. The emperor is the most direct depiction of the concept of the animus, acting as a paternal figure for the people around himself, creating structure and order, and imparting knowledge. He guides his people with a firm hand, performing his role as a source of order above everything else. He rules by serving his people and acting rationally and logically.

Drawing the emperor card in the upright position represents a chance to follow the goals and plans that you have set for yourself, which will allow you to grow and progress as a person. The upright emperor represents to its user a successful and healthy future, as long as they can remember to set goals for themselves and pursue those goals in the same way that the emperor himself does. Another interpretation for the drawing of the emperor card is a current or upcoming position of leadership. This could represent a new position at work or even literal fatherhood. You will need to act as the emperor would, using order and decisiveness, in order to bring clarity and structure to your surroundings.

When the emperor is drawn in the reversed position, however, he represents the abuse of a position of power or authority. This might be something that you have done or will do, or it could be someone close to you. This could be a father figure, possessive partner, or a superior at work who oversteps their role or is performing the role of the emperor inadequately or in a way that betrays the philosophy of the emperor. Regardless of the specifics of your actions, the reversed emperor tells you that you will need to rely more heavily on structure and order in order to find success.

5 – The Hierophant

The fifth card representing another step along the fool's journey is the hierophant. The Hierophant card commonly depicts some sort of religious figure sitting within a church, wearing elaborate vestments in three parts, which are meant to represent three different worlds. The hierophant's right hand is raised upward, likely in the middle of some sort of blessing. This is also the same hand that the magician has raised. In their other hand, the hierophant holds a triple cross, which is a symbol often associated with the pope. The three horizontal bars on the triple cross are thought to represent the Father, the Son, and the Holy Spirit. The hierophant is also commonly depicted along with two acolytes, who represent the transfer of sacred knowledge, and the inclusion of these two acolytes adds to the meaning of the card and draw a line from the hierophant card to the path to gaining knowledge. The hierophant is also called by different names in certain tarot decks, acting as the masculine counterpart to the high priestess. Other names for the hierophant are the high priest and the pope. The hierophant is commonly connected to the role of a guide or a teacher and is commonly associated with the "wise old man" archetype.

When drawn upright, the hierophant represents the embrace of tradition and convention. The hierophant suggests to its recipient that they might want to stay within the conventional path or follow one that has been well-traveled. You might want to stay within certain boundaries of what could be considered normal or typical. Instead of innovating and finding new paths, you will adapt to certain beliefs or certain courses of action that have already been put in place. The hierophant guides people along a typical path. He instructs his recipient that they should "stick to the basics" in order to accomplish their goals. Clichés and tropes exist for a reason, after all. The Hierophant card is typically associated with institutions and their core values. The Hierophant represents the safe and proven routes that will allow you to achieve your goals, as well as moral and ethical norms or traditions.

When the hierophant is drawn in the reversed position, however, he acts as a warning to his recipient that they might be feeling a little bit too restricted or constrained, held down by structures and rules. The reversed Hierophant warns the recipient that they might have lost some of their own action and cannot reach their full potential if they continue on their current path. You might have a strong will and require freedom and the ability to act in your own way. Breaking away from tradition and trying new or unorthodox approaches to your problems will allow you to achieve your goals. The reversed Hierophant, more than anything, instructs their recipient to take action and to challenge tradition in order to act in the ways that suit them and allow them to realize their potential.

6 – The Lovers

The sixth card representing another step along the fool's journey is the lovers. The lovers card commonly depicts a man and a woman being guarded by an angel above them. They are also sometimes depicted as similar to Adam and Eve. Both of the lovers typically appear to be content and secure and standing in the Garden of Eden. The fruit tree with the snake from the story of Adam and Eve stands behind the woman and acts as a hint toward the fall of humanity into the realm of temptation, as per the story of Adam and Eve. The angel that stands behind the couple is Raphael, the angel of the air. There are also other connections to the air within this card. The zodiac sign which this card is representative of is Gemini, the twins, which is also connected to the element of air. The air is commonly associated with the mind and with communication, which is also considered to be a vital and basic aspect of a healthy relationship with another person. The lovers are commonly associated with the concepts of balance, harmony, partnerships, and union between two opposing forces. This union is also significant since a majority of the cards that come before the lovers in the fool's journey are originally presented in pairs; the emperor and empress and the high pope and high priest. The lovers are representative of the union of the concepts that have been presented in the other cards so far. The lovers are also commonly connected to the concepts of duality and balance, and common archetypes that this card represents are the soul or the combination of the anima and animus.

When drawn upright, the lovers symbolize attraction, harmony, and balance in a current or future relationship. The bond of the lovers and the trust that they have in each other are a source of strength for each of them and allow them to empower each other. The lovers' bond is a strong one and can be indicative of a very strong and close relationship that you have with someone close to you. Another common interpretation of the upright lovers card is the idea of duality, presenting the recipient with a choice between two opposing and mutually exclusive options. This could represent a very important decision that you will need to make and which will change your current situation based on the choice that you make.

When the lovers card is drawn in the reversed position, however, they can represent a source of imbalance or discord that exists within your life. These harmful forces can make life incredibly difficult and can even begin to place unnecessary pressure on your relationships with the people around you. You might be struggling with a particular event or choice that you have made, and need to let go of. You should take your own personal values into account in order to understand the problems that you are facing and how to find peace for yourself. The lovers presented in reverse can also represent a relationship that has been broken or cut off, or it can be a source of imbalance between you and the people around you. These problems need to be addressed in order for you to achieve a sense of balance again.

7 – The Chariot

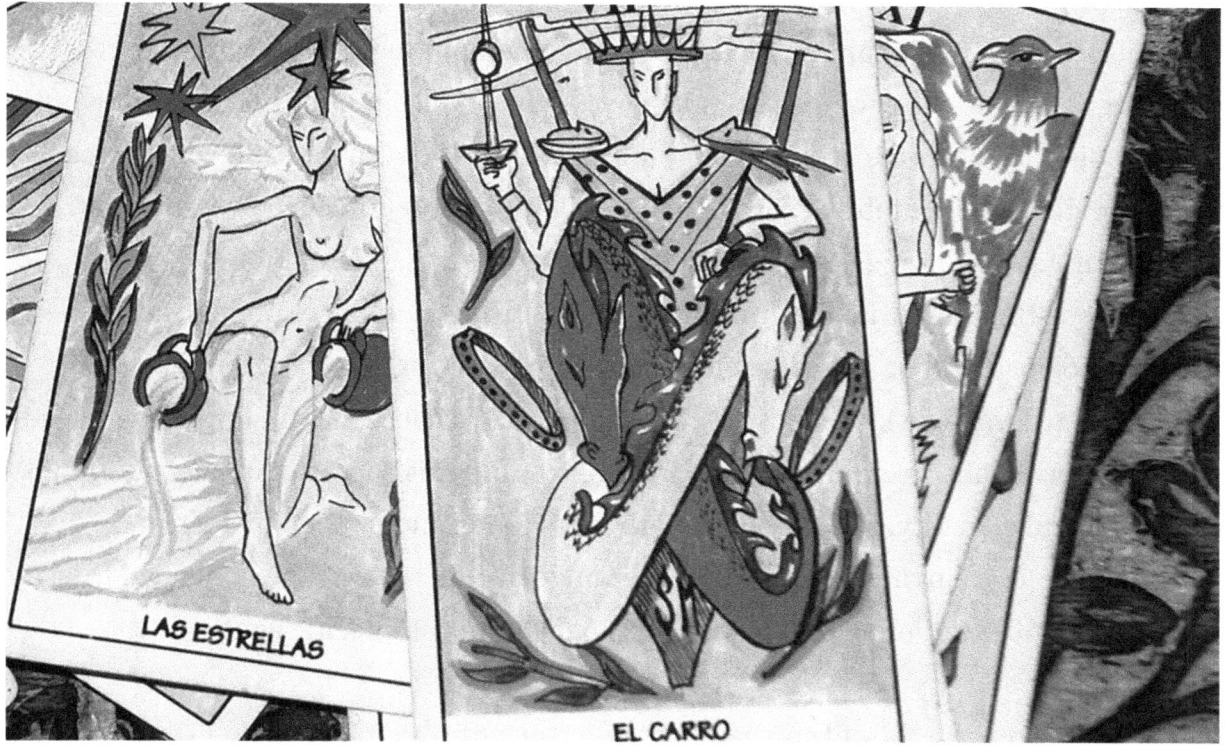

The next card representing another step along the fool's journey is the chariot. The chariot card typically depicts a figure who sits within a vehicle, usually a chariot, which is being pulled by two sphinxes—one black and one white. The chariot is commonly topped with a blue canopy patterned with white stars and wearing armor with lunar symbols on his person. The chariot represents the spiritual guidance that he receives and is influenced by. He typically wears some sort of crown, as well, showing that he has been "enlightened" and that his intentions are pure. The sphinxes that pull the chariot are black and white, representing two opposing forces that the recipient will need to learn to control. The two sphinxes will often try to move in opposing directions, and the chariot will need to guide them forward in order to arrive at his desired destination. The chariot is commonly associated with concepts like hard work, determination, and willpower, as well as control and direction. He is commonly associated with the "warrior" archetype.

The chariot accomplishes his goals and overcomes obstacles that lie in his way by gaining control of the world around him. He maintains confidence in his ability to control his situation and manipulate the forces around him in order to achieve victory. To the recipient, this card being drawn upright might represent opposing or otherwise chaotic or discordant forces around you that you will need to handle with confidence and determination, maintaining focus on manipulating those forces in order to stay on the path that you have set. If you have a particular course of action in mind, you will need to pursue that plan with determination and a strong plan of action in order to reach your goals. It will be important for you to have a strong will in order to achieve your goals, but if you can stay focused, you will be able to succeed. You might even need to discover new qualities within yourself in order to find this success. Anger can often be seen as a negative quality, but the chariot attempts to remind us that it can also be helpful and even synonymous with willpower and drive. It can even be beneficial to those who are able to contain and focus their anger toward a specific goal.

When drawn in reverse, however, the chariot instructs the recipient to do just that. The recipient of the reversed chariot might have a strong will but too little focus to wield it effectively. The reversed chariot represents the sphinxes running out of control and warns the recipient of similarly discordant forces around them, preventing them from finding success. You will need to focus these forces in order to gain control of your surroundings and reach the goals that you are struggling to achieve.

8 – Strength

The next card representing another step along the fool's journey is referred to as "strength." The strength card usually depicts a woman who stands above a male lion, holding its jaws, appearing to be calming the lion and having some sort of power over the beast. A common thing that people will notice regarding the woman depicted on the strength card is how calmly she seems to be handling this fearsome beast. The strength card represents the ability to remain calm and controlled in the face of adversity. She also represents the ideas of bravery and courage, as well as compassion. A common archetype that is associated with strength is "endurance."

The strength card, when drawn in the upright position, shows the strength and fortitude of the recipient, as well as their ability to maintain calmness in stressful or difficult situations. The strength card represents this ability in its recipient and tells them that if they are able to maintain this calmness, they will be able to come out of stressful situations, unharmed. The strength card also tells its recipient about the importance of compassion and consideration for the people and things around you. You should always be able to make time for other people. The strength card also represents the patience of the recipient and their ability to come out on top by utilizing this patience, as well as their fortitude to ensure their safety. The strength that this card refers to is not literal physical strength but inner strength and the ability to persevere or endure. You should also have no issue speaking your mind when you feel strongly about something. You are a passionate person, and you should never attempt to hide that.

When drawn in reverse, however, the strength card indicates that you are currently in some sort of intense anger or fear in your life. Or, it could mean that you will soon encounter a similar challenge. The reversed strength card tells its recipient that they lack the inner strength that this card represents. You might also be lacking in happiness or passion and will need to discover or even rediscover your passion in order to move forward. The reversed strength card might also indicate that you are experiencing depression for any number of different reasons, and you will need to move past it in order to find happiness. You will need to become a more confident and fulfilled person in order to rediscover your strength and become "whole" again.

9 – The Hermit

The next card representing another step along the fool's journey is referred to as the hermit. The hermit card usually depicts an old man standing alone at the top of a mountain, holding a staff in his left hand and a lantern in the right. The mountain is commonly accepted as a representation of the development and success that the hermit has achieved throughout his years. The hermit has gained a large amount of spiritual wisdom throughout his long life and is willing to share that knowledge with others in order to help them grow. The hermit is also deeply committed to the path that he is taking toward his goals. Inside his lantern is also another symbol of wisdom, a six-point star known as the Seal of Solomon. The hermit seeks knowledge and wisdom that comes from within, and he wanders at night searching for that wisdom through prolonged periods of solitude and introspection. In order to understand this path and his goals, the hermit separates himself from others to avoid influences that could possibly affect the words of his inner voice and his ability to hear those words. The hermit represents the exploration of the unconscious for the sake of understanding oneself. Common concepts that are associated with the hermit are contemplation, introspection, and isolation, as well as the search for truth. Similar to the hierophant or high priest, the hermit is representative of the "wise old man" archetype.

The hermit seeks knowledge and wisdom through introspection. He searches through his unconscious for his inner voice, which will tell him about himself and his truths. Drawing the hermit card in the upright position might mean that you need to be alone for a period of time in order to look inward. Introspection can be very important to your personal growth and development. You should never be afraid to spend some time alone and clear your mind of all of the struggles and distractions that come with normal, everyday life. The hermit instructs his recipient that they should also try to be "authentic" and act according to their "true self." The hermit might represent a search for guidance or help with a decision that you do not understand. In some contexts, the hermit might represent the appearance of a person who will act as a mentor to you and provide guidance.

When drawn in reverse, however, the hermit will represent your desire to be alone; maybe you are constantly surrounded by others and need some time to be alone and do some introspection. You should not feel bad about that; everyone needs to take some time for themselves and recover from time to time. However, you should also be careful, as too much "alone time" can become harmful and detrimental to your growth, stunting you in some ways. Isolation can lead to boredom or even madness, causing you to dwell on past events and "losing yourself" or becoming out of touch with reality. The reversed hermit warns against these extremes and reminds the recipient that it is important to maintain a good balance in order to grow and develop as a person.

10 – The Wheel of Fortune

The card holding the number ten, which, of course, represents the tenth step in the fool's journey through the major arcana, is the wheel of fortune. The wheel of fortune is very commonly considered to be one of the most symbolically charged cards within the major arcana and even in the tarot deck as a whole. The image on this card primarily features a very large wheel at its center, which is also covered in a number of different symbols and icons. There are also four creatures that are commonly represented on the face of this card, resting on clouds that surround the wheel of fortune at each of the four corners of the card. These creatures are typically the angel, the bull, the eagle, and the lion. These creatures are related to, and representative of, four of the twelve astrological signs. These are the "fixed" signs, which are Taurus, Leo, Scorpio, and Aquarius. These four beings are also often used to represent the four evangelists within Christianity, which is why they all have wings as well. The books that each being holds in their hands are used to represent of the Torah, which is a collection of the laws of the Lord as they were presented to Moses and recorded as the first five books of the Tanakh, which is the collection of 24 books that make up all of the canonical Hebrew scriptures. The Torah communicates concepts related to wisdom and understanding, and provide the groundwork for the rest of the teachings of the Lord. There is also a snake that is typically depicted on the face of this card, which represents a descent into the "material world," an a sphinx, which sits on the top of the wheel holding a sword, as well as a creature that is usually depicted as either a devil or as the Egyptian god Anubis, who is rising up from the bottom of the card. The sphinx and Anubis are used to represent the wisdom of kings and of the gods, as well as the underworld in the case of Anubis. These two entities rotate eternally as the wheel of fortune spins and carries them along with it, suggesting a fluctuating and opposing relationship between the two beings and the concepts and ideas that they represent. As the sphinx rises to the top of the wheel, Anubis is forced to descend, and vice versa. They cannot rise to the top at the same time, and the rising of one means the descent of the other.

The wheel of fortune is always turning, carrying these two opposing entities along with it at opposite ends, which is representative of the way that life is made up of a variety of different experiences that come and go in phases that exist in a mutually exclusive and alternating pattern. This is true for all living beings. The wheel of fortune represents this duality. When this card is presented in the upright position with the sphinx at the tip of the wheel, it reminds its recipient to make sure to take advantage of the "good times" when they present themselves because they will eventually fall away to make room for "negative" experiences in order to restore balance and continue the eternal turning of the wheel of fortune. Of course, the same is true of the opposite; when you are experiencing the "bad times," it is important to recognize that these experiences will not last forever and that you will need to continue to endure in order to reach the more positive phase of the wheel's turning again. These phases can also be thought of as similar to the turning of the earth and the seasons that come with it. Some people might not particularly like winter and will look forward to spring and summer when they can enjoy the warm weather again. The forces that turn the wheel of fortune are the same forces that govern the passage of time and the seasons, as well as the cycle of day and night.

When the wheel of fortune card is presented in the reversed position, it represents the "bad" phase of the wheel's turning. Luck has not been on your side recently. You are very likely in the middle of the negative phase of the wheel, and it will be important for you to continue to maintain your endurance, waiting for the dawn to come again when the wheel begins to shine in your favor during its next phase. The reversed wheel of fortune instructs its recipient to avoid pretending that they have control over their "luck." The lesson that this card attempts to teach its recipient is that it is best to "let go" and coast during these low points, saving their energy to make the most of the next phase of the wheel's spin when fortune favors them again. If you continue to try to maintain control, reversing, or advancing the spin of the wheel of fortune, it will only bring you more suffering. It might negatively affect the situation that you currently find yourself in. By learning to accept your current situation, you can begin to "move on" in the same way that the wheel does, moving forward in our lives and on our paths to growth and development.

11 – Justice

The 11th step along the fool's journey through the major arcana is represented by the justice card. This is also the 11th numbered major arcana card. The justice card is representative of the concepts of fairness and law, as well as truth and facts. The truth card most commonly depicts an image on its face of a woman sitting in a chair and holding a set of scales in her left hand, which is used to symbolize the justice system and the way that logic should be balanced by intuition. The concepts of logic and intuition can also be thought of as the personal conscious and unconscious minds as well; these two aspects of the mind will need to be balanced for "the fool" to continue to grow and develop and unlock his potential, becoming a unified, whole person again. Justice also carries a double-edged sword in her right hand held up in the air. This represents the duality and the "double-edged" nature of justice and the concepts that she embodies. She also wears a crown atop her head with a square on it, drawing a connection to the element of earth and to clarity, grounded nature, and rigidity that are commonly associated with the element of earth.

When the justice card is drawn in the upright position, she represents the laws of justice. Every decision that you make and every action that you choose to take will have some sort of consequences, whether those consequences are positive or negative. If you have been wronged or you might believe that you are at fault for someone else having been wronged, then the upright justice card tells you that you will not be "punished" for the actions that you have taken or that you will receive some sort of relief. Another common interpretation of the justice card is that it represents the truth. In a situation when the truth might be obfuscated or otherwise concealed or hidden, the truth card tells you that the truth will eventually be revealed or that it needs to be revealed for the situation to be resolved. The truth is based on facts, and you should always be aware of the objective facts that are relevant to your decision before you pass any sort of judgment regarding that situation. You will need to take care and actively seek out the truth in order to maintain fairness in any judgment that you pass. Regardless of the specifics, the truth card presented in the upright position tells its recipient of the importance of objectivity and fairness.

When the justice card is presented in the reversed position, however, it serves to warn its recipient that they are ignoring the truth or "living a lie" in some form or another. This means that you might be thinking objectively or judging someone or something based on your feelings while ignoring the facts of the matter. You might be unwilling to accept the consequences of your actions, falsely believing yourself to be innocent or "running from your guilt." You will need to remember that all actions have consequences and that people make errors sometimes. In order to move forward, you will need to accept the consequences of the actions that you have taken, and you will need to realize that those actions are in the past and learn from the mistakes that you have made. Every new moment presents new opportunities for change and growth, and you can tip the "scales" of justice back in your favor by keeping these lessons in mind. The most significant change that this card advises you to take is to stop unfairly judging yourself, whether you are judging too harshly or not harshly enough. Let yourself be judged by fate. Instead, accept the consequences of your actions, and use those consequences to learn and grow as a person, allowing yourself to move forward.

12 – **The Hanged Man**

The 12th card and the 12th step along the fool's journey through the major arcana is called the "hanged man." The hanged man card most commonly depicts a man who has been suspended upside down from his foot from the world tree. The world tree is typically thought to support the heavens themselves and is rooted in the "underworld," providing a structure for the mortal world. Some versions of the tarot will show the hanged man being suspended upside-down on an inverted cross, in the same way that Saint Peter requested to be hanged, not believing himself to be worthy of the same method of hanging as Jesus Christ. Supporting this interpretation of the hanged man card, many people believe that the hanged man has been placed in the position of his own free will, partially because of the calm and serene expression that he carries on his face. This would make sense if the hanged man were used to represent Saint Peter, as he himself requested to be hanged upside-down and would have accepted his fate by that point. The hanged man is also commonly shown to be bound by only one food, with his right foot being held to the branches of the tree (or to his cross), and the left foot is left free. The hanged man also holds his hands behind his back, possibly also bound, in a triangular shape. He wears red pants, which are symbolic of passion and the physical body, and a blue shirt which represents the seemingly opposed and contrasted concept of peace and calmness. This color combination is also commonly worn by saints, and this would also support the theory that the hanged man represents Saint Peter, or at least that he is a saint. The hanged man also has yellow hair, a yellow halo, and yellow shoes in the most common depictions, representing a high level of intelligence. The hanged man is commonly used to symbolize concepts, such as sacrifice, and is also connected to the archetype of "sacrifice."

The hanged man understands and accepts his situation and recognized that his sacrifice is one that needs to be made in order for him to move forward. The hanged man has likely been sentenced to this fate as a result of wrongs that he has committed in the past or is a calculated sacrifice that he has made in order to allow himself to move forward once his sentence has been completed. While it might seem like his progress has not been halted, the time that is spent on this "step" along his journey is not going to waste. The "hanged man" stage of the fool's journey is a necessary part of his progression. It will allow him to repent for the wrongs that he might have committed or reevaluate his path in order to recalculate and correct himself. This stage comes directly after the "justice" stage, representing this repentance, as well. The hanged man can also be used to represent a "new perspective," as the hanged man is literally upside down and will have an opportunity to begin to view the world through a different lens, gaining a new sense of perspective regarding the world around them. Other people around the hanged man who is close to him might not understand this part of his journey or the sacrifice that he needs to make. They might even protest against his sentence, but the hanged man will be able to view his situation differently and accept that his sacrifice is necessary for his own growth, as well as the growth of his peers, in some cases. When the hanged man is presented in the upright position, he might tell his recipient of the need to suspend or stop a certain course of action or to reevaluate the current path that they are taking. Certain actions or plans might need to be put off for a while or even stopped altogether for you to progress successfully. The hanged man will instruct his recipient to stop and reflect on their current plans or actions, adopting a new method in order to achieve success. Another important lesson that the hanged man can teach is to wait. Stopping to understand your situation and the outcomes of your actions, waiting until the optimal moment to act will allow you to find success much more easily. In some situations, taking action at the first opportunity might even have negative consequences and prevent you from reaching your goals, and waiting can sometimes be more beneficial.

In the reversed position, the hanged man might represent the failure to listen to his lessons. You might be acting relentlessly and without hesitation, failing to understand the consequences of your actions later on, or you might be pushing toward a goal that is unattainable, at least with the method that you are currently using. You might be doing a lot of work for little to no reward, and it will be important for you to stop and evaluate your situation in order to think of a new approach.

13 – Death

The 13th card and step along the fool's journey through the major arcana is the death card. Death is commonly depicted as the entity known as "death," one of the four horsemen of the apocalypse, resembling an armored skeleton riding a horse and carrying a flag in his hand through what appears to be a battlefield. The figure that is portrayed on the death card is depicted as a skeleton representing his role, as the bones are the last part of the human body to continue existing after they have died. Death also wears armor in a lot of common versions of the tarot, which is symbolic of his invulnerability. He is protected against attacks, unlike most of the other figures portrayed within the tarot. This is connected to death's role in the cycle of life as a concept that will always be following us throughout our lives. Nobody can kill death; it is simply a fact. The white horse that death rides also represents the concept of purity, which is closely related to death as a "purifying" force that will eventually affect every living thing. On one hand, he carries a flag with a black base and a white pattern, usually drawn as a flower of some sort. Death rides his horse through a battlefield filled with dead or dying humans in the dirt. Most versions of this card will show both a king and a pauper in the dirt at death's mercy, representing his objectivity and the way that he does not judge anyone based on their race, class, gender, or any other fabricated symbol of superiority or inferiority that humans and other animals tend to judge each other by. Death eventually comes for all living things when their time has come. Some common concepts that are associated with the death card are change, transition, and rebirth. Death is also associated with the "rebirth" archetype, as well.

Many people tend to misunderstand or even fear death as a result of their perspective coming from the point of view of a creature that has not yet experienced it. Similarly, the death card is also considered "bad" or "unlucky," and its number of 13 certainly does not help with the way it is perceived. A lot of people might even avoid mentioning this card because of their fear of the concept of death and the way that most people will interpret this card, representing literal death. This is false, however. Death can sometimes have one of the most positive meanings of the major arcana cards and even the tarot deck as a whole. The death card, when it is presented in the upright position, represents that one phase of your life is ending and that a new one is about to begin. This is the "halfway point" along the fool's journey, and it might even be represented in the "hero's journey" as the climax of the story. This is the point after which the "hero" would have suffered a massive defeat against the villain and would have found a new drive, being inspired again to finally defeat the antagonist. In terms of typical human life and experiences, this card might manifest as a new job or finishing your time at school in order to move on to begin your career in your chosen field of work. It can also be the end of a long-term relationship that will make room for your "true love" if this change or transition occurs within your romantic life. Regardless of the specifics, the death card represents the end of one phase and the transition to another, similar to the transition from life to death in the journey of human existence. You will need to "let go" of the phase of your life that is coming to an end in order to recognize and embrace the new one that is or will be presenting itself to you.

Another common interpretation of the death card is that the transformation or transition that it represents will be within yourself. You might be undergoing some sort of transformation or "metamorphosis," and you will need to allow your "old self" to "die" in order to make room within yourself for the "new you" to develop. This can often be a scary or daunting period and is usually the cause of some sort of significant life event, but it is usually for the better, allowing you to become a "new person" in order to grow and develop in this "new path" that you will be traveling in the next phase of your life. You will need to embrace this new phase and let go of unhealthy attachments that you might have developed previously in order to move on. This is a very important part of life and will likely occur multiple times throughout a person's journey as they learn and develop throughout their life.

When the death card is presented in the reversed position, it still represents change. However, it might warn you that you have been resisting a significant change in your life, and you will need to begin to embrace it in order to move forward. You might be worried about letting go of your past due to an attachment to aspects of your past that you are still hanging on to, or you might even be unsure or ignorant of the new phase of your life and the opportunities that have been presenting themselves to you. You will need to take time to evaluate and assess the aspects of your past that you are trying to hang on to and begin to let them go so that you can continue to grow and develop. Much like the wheel of fortune, life is constantly moving forward, and any attempt to stop that progress or move backward along the wheel will only be detrimental to you in the long run.

14 – Temperance

The 14th card and step along the fool's journey through the major arcana is the "temperance" card. The temperance card commonly depicts an image of a winged angel, with no obvious gender, which is used to represent a balance between the sexes. The angel stands with one foot in the water of a pond, which symbolizes their unconscious mind, while their left foot rests on dry land as a representation of their connection to their conscious mind and to the material world. The angel wears a white robe with the image of a triangle inside a square, drawing another connection between the physical, material world and the divine or the holy trinity. Temperance also holds two cups, mixing water between the two cups. A lot of people will also believe these two cups to be representative of the conscious and unconscious minds. Balance is an important theme in this card, and it represents the harmony that comes from the union of dual opposed forces, similar to the forces that have been represented in a number of the cards of the major arcana up to this point in the fool's journey. Common concepts that are associated with the temperance card are balance, moderation, and the union of opposites.

When the temperance card is presented in the upright position, it tells its recipient that they might have a good handle on the lessons that they teach. You might be able to maintain balance well and even maintain control and calmness in times of stress. Being able to remain calm in stressful situations, maintain control, and not let the "little things" bother you can be extremely valuable skills that will help you in achieving any goals that you set for yourself. Temperance instructs their recipients to maintain balance in all aspects of life. Moving toward the extreme in any situation, especially in sensitive situations, should be avoided if possible. The temperance card also suggests that its recipient likely has a clear drive and a specific vision, understanding exactly what they are aiming for. This is important in achieving your goals, as you will be able to understand each of the steps that need to be taken in order to reach them. Understanding the temperance card's lessons will be useful in helping you to find "peace" within yourself and situations that you might find yourself in. The temperance card might also be telling you that it is time to reevaluate and assess the situation and your priorities. Being able to find some sort of balance between your inner self and the outside world will allow you to find a much greater purpose and live a much more fulfilling and satisfying life.

When the temperance card is presented in reversed order, it might represent some kind of imbalance somewhere in your life that is causing you some sort of stress or anxiety. The specifics of this imbalance will often be revealed through the other cards in your spread. Temperance can also serve as a warning against a specific path or course of action. That will force you to lean on an extreme and will cause an imbalance in your life in the near future. You might also be in danger of suffering from a lack of drive or purpose. The primary lesson that temperance teaches is that balance and moderation should be maintained at all times and that it is important to stop and consider our actions and our lives to make sure to maintain that balance as much as we can.

15 – The Devil

The 15th card and 15th step along the fool's journey through the major arcana is the devil card. The devil card most commonly depicts a demon or an evil in a very satyr-like form. It is commonly thought that the creature represented on this card is Baphomet. He is half-goat and half-man and has two unsettling bat wings, as well as an inverted pentagram on his forehead. He stands on top of a pedestal behind a nude man and woman who are chained to the pedestal, showing that he has some sort of control over these two people. Both the man and the woman also have horns, which are representative of their sinful and sub-human nature, which they have adopted after a long period of time spent in service of the devil. The chains that bind them give the impression that they have been imprisoned or otherwise taken captive by the devil. Both of these people also have a tail, as well. The man's tail has a flame at its end, while the woman's tail has a cluster of grapes at the end of her tail, representing their respective addictions to power and the "finer" things in life. Of course, if you look at the expression of the man and the woman's faces, you would see that they look very displeased because they have been stripped of their power and status when they were taken hostage by the devil and left exposed and naked as a sign of shame.

The devil card is very different from the rest of the cards that have led up to it so far in that its meanings are reversed. The upright devil's appearance in your reading might reveal feelings of entrapment or restriction that you are experiencing or even lacking satisfaction or fulfillment within your life. You might also be distracted by materialism and drawn from your path by greed or similar struggles in a similar manner to the man and the woman shown on the face of the devil card. You might even be aware that the path that you walk on is a sinful and dangerous one, but you do not seem to have control over your hunger or greed. This card can often be used to represent a struggle with addiction to substances like drugs, alcohol, or even food, as well as greed and materialism. In these kinds of situations, you might feel a lack of control or that you are unable to control your impulses, directing yourself toward anything other than these impure desires. Drawing the devil card in your reading might mean that you need to break free from these bonds and begin to walk a pure path again, or you might risk becoming a "slave" to these desires like the man and woman on this card.

Drawing the devil card in its reversed position is also somewhat "backward," holding the "positive" interpretation of this card unlike the rest of the cards of the major arcana, which represent positive lessons when they are presented in the upright position and negative lessons when they are drawn reversed, requiring some form of adjustment or change from the recipient in order to move forward on their path to growth and development. Drawing the devil card in its reversed position, however, represents the moment when an individual is able to recognize their addictions and break free of the bonds that hold them captive. This might represent something like overcoming an addiction to drugs or alcohol or even something like breaking "bad habits" that you might have formed over time and beginning to recover from the damage that those things have caused to you.

Usually, this turn comes from a moment of self-awareness or becoming exhausted with the way you have been moving, recognizing that the path you walk is harmful to your growth or that you have been turned around and begun to walk backward and will need to turn around again in order to move forward again. Regardless of the specifics of your situation, being able to break your "bonds" and let go of your addictions or vices is always difficult, and you will need to be able to make all of the changes that are necessary, regardless of how scary or painful they are in order to continue walking on the "correct path." While the reversed death card still instructs its recipient that they will need to make some sort of change in their life, it is the more "positive" orientation of this card and presents an opportunity to change their negative habits and recover from them, as opposed to simply being a warning against a negative course of action that will need to be corrected.

16 – The Tower

The next step along the fool's journey along the major arcana is the 16th numbered card, which is referred to as the tower. The tower card commonly depicts a tall tower that rests at the top of a high mountain. The tower is also usually shown being struck by lightning, which also sets the tower on fire, causing panic in the people inside the tower.

The windows of this tower burst with flames, including the people who used to be inside the tower, who have jumped, at this point, out of the windows. These people are likely the same people who can be seen in the other cards of the major arcana, like the devil or the lovers, and possibly the people in the paired cards, like the emperor and empress. The people are jumping from the windows of their tower in the act of desperation, wishing to escape the destruction of the tower and the chaos that is caused by it. The tower card is most often used to represent ambition that is built on shaky or unstable foundations, as well as things like change or destruction as a form of creation. The tower needs to be destroyed and broken down for it to be cleared out to make room for new things to exist in its place. It is also likely going to serve as part of the foundation for whatever ends up being built in its place. The tower card is commonly associated with concepts like forceful change or a sudden upheaval or some sort of chaos or disaster that is unexpected or unwanted. A common archetype for this card is "chaos."

The tower card represents extreme change. This card is specifically designed to be very dark and to look very differently from a lot of the cards that have come earlier in the journey of the fool. Its design primarily features an object, as opposed to a person or creature, that is being attacked in a very dark background. The tower is the first card in the major arcana that illustrates an event, especially one so violent and destructive, as well. The crown that calls from the top of the tower is meant to paint the tower as some sort of a symbol of power, and as it is being destroyed, that symbol and that power go with it, enforcing the theory that the man and the woman featured in the image on this card are the same man and woman featured in the devil card. This card represents change much more directly than any of the other cards in the major arcana and even in the tarot deck as a whole. This card very directly represents a deep, foundational change to the person who draws it in their tarot reading. However, this event does not necessarily need to be a destructive, unpleasant, or a terrible disaster like lightning and fire, which are featured on the face of this card. It is usually violent or extreme, however. Despite change being such a very important part of life that all people and things experience, many people do not handle change very well and will rather cling to the normalcy that is provided by the lives that they are used to, even if the change that is occurring in their life is a positive one or will provide benefits to that person. Even if the change that they are experiencing is positive, they might respond with fear because of reasons similar to those that are mentioned in the section on the death card. You will need to abandon your previous situation or truths, or "abandoning the tower," in order to embrace your new situation, but whether this change is positive or negative, it will be beneficial in the long run. Life only moves forward, and embracing change will allow you to move forward as a person and grow in the way that the fool's journey is intended to represent.

When the tower card is presented in the upright position, it tells you that you might be experiencing a significant change in your life soon or at the current time with positivity and eagerness. This period of change might create some sort of tension between you and the people who are involved with you. Because of this, you will need to remain calm in order to maintain control and transition smoothly to this new stage. In the context of work or interpersonal relationships, this might mean that you will need to be objective and calm, making sure not to lose your temper or be heavily emotionally affected. You need to meditate to prevent inadvertently hurting the people around you during this stressful or unfamiliar time.

When the tower is presented in the reversed position, this might mean that a significant change will be coming soon. This change is commonly interpreted as negative, taking the form of a stressful or unwanted crisis that will cause trouble for you or those around you. You might want to try to delay this event, but you should, instead, try to embrace the change that comes; even if they are unpleasant, painful, or harmful to you at the moment, these kinds of events can be incredibly beneficial to you in the long run. More often than not, these changes will serve to destroy or break negative habits or reliance on habits or things that are detrimental to your personal development. The "tower" or this reliance is built on weak foundations, and it will need to fall in order to be rebuilt as something more stable.

17 – The Star

The 17th card and the 17th step along the fool's journey through the major arcana is referred to as the star. The star card commonly depicts a nude blonde woman kneeling at the edge of a small pond, which is similar to the pond that the figure in the temperance card stands above. The woman on the star card is also similar to the woman on the face of the temperance card, as she also holds two containers with water in them. Instead of cups, however, the woman holds two much larger vessels, which more closely resemble jugs. One of these jugs is pouring its contents out onto the land, filling it with water, and nourishing the dry land in order to encourage fertility and growth. The land that surrounds the star seems to indicate that pouring water into the soil seems to be working, judging by the healthy field that surrounds her. In a similar manner to temperance, the star also has one foot immersed in the water of her pond, representing her spiritual abilities and her inner strength. The other food is firmly planted on the land to represent her connection with the material world. Behind the woman, there is a large star that is also surrounded by seven smaller white stars. Each of these stars represents a different chakra or "spiritual center" that exists within the body, with the largest likely being used to represent the star herself. Far behind the star in the field stands a single tree, with a bird perched on top of it. This bird is meant to represent the wisdom of Thoth. Some common concepts that are associated with the star card are faith and hope, and an archetype that is connected to this card is, of course, referred to as "the star."

The star represents hope, faith, and inner strength when it is drawn in the upright position. This card follows the trauma and the change that is presented in the tower card, and it represents the strength that is needed in order to handle the change that is described in that card's meaning. Following that significant period of change or trauma, it might not necessarily be immediately apparent, but the star card lets you know that you have not been forgotten by "the universe" and that you will need to endure difficulty in this trying time. When you come out of this period, you will come out much stronger than before and with all of the tools that you need in order to reach your goals. The star also tries to instruct its recipient that they will need to have faith and be courageous in these difficult times, and the universe will bless them with the strength that they need in order to succeed. When you draw this card in a tarot reading, it represents some sort of challenge or difficult experience that you have had recently in your life. It also means that you have managed to go through it without losing your hope. While you very likely suffered in some way or another because of this event, you managed to come out of it relatively okay. You might have even learned that you are stronger than you thought yourself to be, and this traumatic event has helped you to understand your inner strength and potential.

If you draw the star card in the reversed position, however, this might represent a loss of faith regarding a recent traumatic or otherwise stressful or trying situation. You might be feeling like everything is hopeless or that you do not have the strength that you need. These challenges might normally be something that you would look forward to, but for some reason, you have lost faith and begun to second-guess yourself. This loss of faith or "strength" has most likely been caused by a change in your perception of either yourself or of something that you hold dear and which is a large part of your inner strength. When you lose faith in something that is so important to you and who you are, it becomes incredibly difficult to continue to move forward or find the motivation to do anything at all. Sometimes, this might manifest as anxiety, depression, or any other number of psychological disorders that occur as a result of trauma. In order to begin to move past this difficult or traumatic event, you need to evaluate your feelings and understand them. You need to understand why you might be experiencing this defeat or why you are experiencing this loss of faith. The reversed star instructs its recipient to take care of their mental health and nurture it in a healthy way that allows them to find their faith and rebuild their strength.

18 – The Moon

The next step along the fool's journey through the major arcana is the 18th card, which is referred to as "the moon." The moon card most commonly depicts a scene that features the literal moon. The moon rests at the top of the image on this card, above a path that leads off into the horizon. On each side of this path at the center of the card are a wolf and a dog. These two animals represent the nature of human beings, split between one part that is civilized and domesticated, and one that is wild and feral. The path comes from a pond at the bottom of this card's image, and a crawfish is also shown to be coming out of that pond. Off in the distance, the scene also shows two towers set at the opposite ends of the path, drawing another connection to duality and opposing forces. Everything in this card seems to be a mirror image of its other side, in the same way that the moon reflects the light of the sun. These mirrored images also represent choices between two divergent paths, which is a very common theme with the tarot's major arcana. Walking the path that is depicted in this card requires us to maintain a balance between the conscious and the unconscious mind, or between the wild and civilized aspects of ourselves, as they are represented by the wolf and the dog, respectively. Additionally, the towers on either side of the moon's path are also representative of the forces of good and evil. Which tower is meant to represent which concept is intentionally left unclear, and this is likely in an effort to obfuscate the differences between these forces at a surface level and highlighting the similarities between the two. These two forces can often be difficult to tell apart since good and evil are largely subjective concepts, with morality being a large grey area. The line between the two is a very thin one, which might be represented by the path between these two towers. The moon card is commonly associated with feelings and emotions.

When the moon card is presented in an upright position, it can be symbolic of the imagination. It might mean that your imagination is running out of control and getting the better of you, similarly to when you are walking along a dark path at night, you might be unsure of your surroundings, wary of danger that lurks in the shadows and stalks you, waiting for an opportune moment to lunge and attack you. In this situation, you will be represented by the crawfish, which is rising up out of the water and is at the beginning of the moon card's path. To you, the crawfish, the moon will be a source of light and will bring you a sense of clarity and understanding. You should follow the moon or your intuition, allowing it to guide you through this darkness and carry you to safety. You will also need to consider the fear or unease that you are experiencing and keep them in mind. More often than not, these feelings are based on input from the outside world or from our unconscious minds trying to tell us something about our surroundings or our situation. Another common interpretation of the moon card is that it represents illusions or deception. You will need to look past the shadows or unpleasant feelings that you might have in order to discover the truth.

When the moon card is drawn in the reversed position, it can be interpreted as a representation of the dark, negative aspects of the moon, which represents your intuition or unconscious mind. The reversed moon card might be representative of feelings of unease or confusion that you might be feeling. You might want to move forward, but you are unsure of which direction to move or which path to take. You will need to move past these unpleasant feelings and look past the shadows along your path in order to discover the truth along the "correct" path. Another common interpretation of the reversed moon card is that the forces of the night bringing you confusion are starting to dissipate. You have started managing your fears and anxiety. Whatever negative energies you have been facing are slowly fading away. It presents a liberating experience as you discover the positive side of things.

19 – The Sun

The next stage of the fool's journey through the major arcana is the 19th numbered card, which is referred to as the sun. The sun card is used to represent feelings like optimism and fulfillment. This card also represents the dawn, which follows the darkest of nights, both in a literal sense and a symbolic one. The sun is the source of all life on our planet; we would not exist without its energy and light. The sun card commonly depicts a child in the image on its surface. This child is shown to be playing in the foreground of this image and is a representation of innocence. This child and its innocence are also symbolic of the happiness that can be felt when you are in alignment with your "true self." The child is also naked, but unlike some other figures that are shown to be naked, like the man and woman in the devil card, this child does not seem to mind. This is representative of the fact that this child is pure and innocent and that there's nothing to hide; this child does not care to hide anything about themselves. This child does not have any shame and simply exists to enjoy their life. This child also rides on the back of a white horse, similar to the one in the Death card. Like the horse that death rides on, this horse is used to represent the concept of purity, as well as the strength and nobility in the context of this card. Common concepts that are associated with this card are joy and positivity, as well as success and achievement.

When the sun card is presented in an upright position, it can be used to represent things like abundance, success, and radiance. Much like the literal celestial body of the sun, the sun card is a symbol of strength and vitality, pouring life into all the people and things that fall within reach of the sun. This is a very positive card, telling its recipient that they will be experiencing easy times of joy and happiness in the very near future. At the time when the fool comes to the sun card's stage of his journey, he would have experienced a great deal of hardship, and the sun card is where the fool will begin to experience the benefits of those hardships much more directly. You have accomplished a lot and grown as a person, and because of your own personal fulfillment, you will often provide other people around you with inspiration and joy as well. A lot of people will be almost magnetically drawn or attracted to you because of the warm and beautiful energy that you bring into their lives with your drive and ambition, as well as your positivity and your kindness. You will also be able to help other people by shifting some of that light and leading it to their direction in order to allow them to grow and flourish, much like plants or animals, as they experience the warmth of the real sun. This card represents a very significant amount of confidence that you have achieved through hard work and perseverance, enduring all the difficulties and overcoming all the obstacles that fell along your path in order to continue growing. Your life will be particularly pleasant and easy. The sun shines on you and will allow you to easily reach the goals that you have set for yourself. While the devil card was singled out as a very unpleasant card for a number of different reasons, the sun card would represent the opposite. The sun card is one of the most positive cards in the tarot, and finding this card in a reading can almost always represent a similar positivity that you carry with you at all times.

In the reversed position, the sun indicates that you might have significant difficulties in finding positive aspects in certain situations. The clouds might be blocking out the warmth and light that you need to progress. This might be preventing you from feeling confident and powerful. You may experience certain setbacks, which are damaging your optimism and enthusiasm. On the other hand, the sun reversed might be indicative that you are unrealistic. It might be a sign that you have an overly optimistic perception of certain situations. These are things that you need to take into account in order to ensure that you are on the right track, and your successes continue as they do.

20 – Judgment

The next step along the fool's journey through the major arcana is the 20th numbered card, which is referred to as "judgment." The judgment card commonly depicts an angel, Gabriel, who sits in the sky playing a trumpet. There are several people who are shown on this card to be rising up from their graves to greet Gabriel, reaching their arms out to show that they are prepared to be judged by the universe or by their gods. These people are likely being pulled from their graves as part of the rapture to have their actions weighed in order to be judged by the universe and find out where they will live for the rest of eternity—in the heavens up above or in hell below. The judgment card also commonly features a large tidal wave coming from the horizon, which is meant to represent a catastrophic event that will eventually come for all the people who still wait for their judgment. That judgment is unavoidable and cannot be changed. The judgment card has a similar meaning as the death card, in the sense that it represents the end of one phase of existence to allow us to move on to the next. The primary difference between the judgment and death cards is the context. Many of the people portrayed in this card or versions of this card have already died and risen from their graves to receive judgment. This card also presents (at least) two paths: heaven and hell. These two paths represent the result of the actions that we have taken and the consequences that those actions will have. Additionally, this card is different from death and most of the other cards in the major arcana because it does not describe an event that is happening or about to happen to its recipient. The judgment card acts as more of a warning, letting its recipient know that they will eventually be judged for their actions and their intentions and that they should keep that in mind when they act. Judgment mentions the transitions that we experience going from life to death, but those transitions are not its main focus; judgment intends to let its recipients know that their actions will have consequences, regardless of the intent behind them. Some common concepts that are associated with the judgment card are awareness, awakening, reflection, completion, and consequences.

The judgment card's original meaning was to help its recipient to begin to reflect on themselves and the actions that they take through this reflection and self-awareness. In order to understand how we will be judged, we will need to gain a clear and objective understanding of where we are now and the ways that our actions will be judged when the time comes. For a lot of people, this understanding will largely come from a moment when we become self-aware and begin to evaluate the actions that we have taken, changing the path where we travel in order to become "better people." This is a very common archetype in film and television and will be easy to understand with the context of characters like Ebenezer Scrooge. The judgment card refers to the moment when we begin to reflect on the paths that we have chosen and the actions that we have taken. This card is used to represent that you might be coming close to "awakening" or that you are in the middle of awakening in your life. It follows that you might soon begin evaluating yourself and your intentions, judging yourself in order to understand what you might need to change and how you might need to alter your path in life. If you are already going through this period of awakening, you might need to move forward and make those changes in your life in order to continue growing and become a better, more spiritually, or mentally healthy person. Not only will this course correction affect you positively in the long run, but the people around you might also end up benefiting from your new outlook.

Ultimately, the judgment card represents moments of clarity that present us with choices that we will need to make in our lives, deciding the direction that we will end up taking toward the future. Sometimes, these moments are irreversible and cannot be altered or changed once they have been made, so it is important to understand all the details and the consequences of these choices in order to make the "correct" one. You will be judged for these actions later on, so it is important to choose your path wisely, but you must choose a path and accept the consequences of that choice either way.

It is important to judge yourself and your actions in order to be self-aware and to understand the choices that you make and why those choices are made, but it is also important to judge yourself accurately. When the judgment card is drawn in the reversed position, it can act as a warning that you might not be judging yourself accurately. You might be too loose with your judgments, not accurately weighing your actions and intentions, or you might even be judging yourself too harshly. This might be causing you to miss out on opportunities that are waiting for you or that have presented themselves to you while you spend too much of your time worrying about the actions that you have taken and the consequences of those actions. This lost momentum can sometimes cause you to fall behind your plans and make it much more difficult to reach the goals that you have set for yourself. You might need to worry less about the consequences of your actions in order to continue moving forward. Of course, you should still be keeping those actions in mind, but you should also remember that, if you focus all of your attention on worrying about the past, you will not be able to focus on the present as effectively. You should be able to move onward proudly and confidently in order to act in a way that is true to yourself.

21 – The World

The last step on the path of the fool's journey through the major arcana is the card with the number 21, referred to as the world. The world card commonly depicts a woman in the center of the image on its face. This woman seems to be dancing, with one leg crossed behind the other as if she were walking or dancing. She holds one wand in each of her hands, placed down at her sides. She is surrounded by a green wreath of flowers that symbolizes her success, and the wreath is wrapped in red ribbons that are meant to appear similar to the infinity symbol. There are also usually four beings in the four corners of this card, which are the same beings that can be seen on the wheel of fortune card. These creatures are representations of a number of different aspects of our universe and our world. Connections can be drawn from these four creatures to the four evangelicals, the four classical elements, the four corners of our universe, and even to astrological symbols. Regardless of the specific interpretation of what these four creatures are, they represent harmony and unification of their energies. These four very different beings all exist together and work in harmony to support the figure depicted in the center of this card. There are a number of different concepts that are commonly associated with the world card, as it represents the unification of all of the lessons and the different aspects of the self that have been discovered and understood by the fool throughout his journey through the major arcana, but some of these concepts include completion, harmony, fulfillment, satisfaction, and wholeness.

Drawing the world card in the upright position often represents a sense of unity and completion in your life, whether that unity is occurring at the time of the reading or will be coming to you in the near future. This card is representative of the inner and outer worlds coming together to become a single entity. In terms of personal growth, this can be thought of as the bridge between the conscious and unconscious minds, or your connection with the world around you. In some traditions, people will refer to this state as "enlightenment" or "nirvana." This is the final stage of your journey, at least mentally and emotionally speaking. This is when you will have recognized that you and all other living things are linked with each other and that we all serve as individual parts of the universe as a whole. Being able to recognize and understand the nature of human existence and life as a whole means that you have completed your spiritual journey and that you are able to be a part of the greater whole that makes up the universe. At this point, you can be considered "whole" again, and you have all the strength and the tools that you will need in order to handle any challenge that might come your way. This card also represents joy, fulfillment, and accomplishment. All the efforts that you have been putting in place are finally beginning to pay off. You have completed a very significant milestone in your life and have gained all the tools that you need in order to move forward.

When the world card is drawn in the reversed position, it can represent the end of a particular journey or era. You may have many accomplishments that have lined your path, but there is a strange emptiness that fills you when you look back upon it as if you have all the pieces, but they are not coming together. In order to continue to move onward, you will need to evaluate yourself and your personal growth in order to understand what is missing or what is preventing you from experiencing the satisfaction that you should be feeling right now. Something is missing and needs to be recovered before you can complete your journey.

Chapter 4: Tarot and the Unconscious

As was discussed briefly in the last chapter of this book, divinatory tarot readings are based on the concepts of Jungian psychology, rather than from magic or some other mystical force that manipulates the cards. The personal and collective unconscious play a very large role in the outcomes of tarot readings. When you read or receive a tarot reading, the cards themselves are not the tool that will provide you with the answers you are looking for. The cards simply act as catalysts, pushing you to look within your unconscious mind by presenting you with concepts from the "collective unconscious," which can be thought of as a level deeper than the "personal unconscious" mind, where all the experiences and archetypes common to all people or to large groups of people can be held. The collective unconscious is simply made up of all the experiences and concepts that are common to many or all people and is more of metaphysical space, rather than a real location or part of the mind.

Being able to access the personal unconscious can sometimes be difficult for different people, depending on how closely they are connected to their unconscious minds. This is because, over time, we have "lost touch" with our inner selves. It could also be because of the way that people have evolved. Modern people tend to ignore their unconscious minds, neglecting the development of these parts of ourselves and, instead, favoring the conscious mind and turning to logic and reasoning in order to help us solve our problems. Most people will tend to look outside themselves and even reach out to other people for the answers and solutions to their problems, which can be harmful to their growth within their unconscious minds. When we fall sick, we will usually go to a doctor or purchase medications that can treat the symptoms of those diseases instead of simply searching for the original cause or source of the issue, like our environment or habits. A large part of our personalities and the things that make us ourselves lie in our unconscious minds. It contains all the information that we do not actively remember but affect us, which can often be more important to our identities than the conscious mind. The unconscious mind forms our "unexplained" habits, our likes and dislikes, and even our dreams. It is said that we experience our unconscious minds and the experiences and thoughts within them through our dreams. This is because when we sleep, our conscious mind also "sleeps" and lets its guard down to allow the unconscious mind to surface.

A lot of people will rely too much on their conscious mind to help them make their decisions and guide them through their everyday lives. Modern-day people rely heavily on their physical senses, focusing primarily on the world around them. When we think of an object, the way we think of that object is primarily influenced by the physical senses that we use to perceive or experience that object, rather than the experiences that we have with that object. Usually, the first method by which we consider specific objects is our sight. Most of the time, this is the first sense that we use to experience a particular object. Before we can feel, smell, or taste something, we will usually see it. There are some exceptions, like objects with strong odors or very loud machines, but normally, we will judge an item based on its physical appearance. However, most of these objects also make some sort of impact on our unconscious minds based on the experiences that we have involving those objects. This is the source of a lot of our fears or habits that we form. Most people have begun to lean more heavily on the outside world and their physical senses and have become imbalanced and unhealthy after losing touch with our unconscious minds as we have developed. Tarot cards, when used for divinatory purposes, push us to try to become closer with our unconscious minds in order to better understand how we function as people and how to solve the issues that we face in our lives.

Some people may be more in tune with their unconscious minds and more aware of when it is "trying to tell them something." Usually, these people will rely much more heavily on intuition than a lot of other people, or they will be a little bit more self-aware, having the ability to acknowledge their quirks and the origins of the aspects of their personalities that they might not otherwise be aware of. Every person has moments throughout their lives when they might be more in tune with their unconscious minds, however. And they simply need to be aware of the messages that they are receiving from their unconscious mind in order to recognize them and understand themselves as a person. Usually, these messages will manifest in the form of "intuition" when you encounter a new person who gives you a creepy or unsettling feeling. For example, one might be trying to make a very important decision and feel inexplicably compelled to choose one option over another. When people say to "listen to your gut," this is usually referring to intuition and the unconscious mind. In this sense, it is true that people only use part of their brain's full capacity because many people fail to recognize that their "gut sense" or "intuition" is a real part of their brain and mind and can provide incredibly valuable insight in times of stress or difficulty, even if we do not completely understand the *why* part at that time.

Tarot cards are designed in a way to rely on imagery and concepts that exist within the "collective unconscious" in order to encourage readers or people who are receiving readings about themselves to reach out to their unconscious mind for guidance. It encourages people to develop a stronger connection to their unconscious mind so that they can learn to rely on it more often and begin to understand themselves better. This will help the reader or recipient of the reading to grow and develop more and become a "whole" person, as Carl Jung believed that every person has the opportunity to do so.

Chapter 5: Tarot and Numerology

Another very important part of the symbolism of tarot cards is the number that is on each card. The major arcana cards each have a number ranging from 0 to 21, and the minor arcana have four suits of 1-10 numbered cards with four cards that do not have numbers. The numbers on the cards can help you to understand various archetypes and aspects of human life, as well as serve as a little bit of a shortcut when performing tarot readings once you know what each number means. Tarot cards have been carefully designed with their numbers in mind. These numbers and their cards were discussed briefly earlier in this book, as well as the concept of the "fool's journey," which outlines the path to mental and emotional growth that the "fool" takes throughout his life. However, the numbers on the minor arcana cards are also helpful and allow us to understand ourselves better in a similar way to the major arcana cards.

Minor Arcana

The minor arcana has a total of 56 cards, split into four groups—swords, coins, cups, and wands. Each of these groups has 10 numbered cards and four "court" cards. These are the king, queen, knight, and page. Most of the time, however, some decks have different variations on the specific roles that the court cards play. Some decks might change out the knight and page cards to be the prince and princess, the jack and knave, or even add two extra cards, the maid and the mounted lady, to act as foils to the knight and page. Again, while there are a lot of cards in the tarot deck, with the most well-known decks containing 78 cards, they can all be split up into much smaller sections with consistent rules. The meanings of the minor arcana's numbered cards are listed here.

1 — This is also known as the ace. The ace card of any suit is the beginning of the numbered progression of that suit's ideals and concepts. As such, the ace cards represent beginnings, new opportunities, and potential. This is the first step in the path to the shorter, simpler journey to the "minor secrets" that the minor arcana holds. These are shorter than the major arcana but still very important, as they represent the paths to understanding the more specific ideals of the four suits of the minor arcana. The ace can be thought of like the introduction to the concepts and ideals of the four suits. This introduction might come in the form of inspiration regarding a particular art or field of study, or even as something like recognizing your career goals or receiving an opportunity to move into your desired field of work or study. This first step is all about beginnings and new opportunities.

2 — The second step along this journey is the 2 cards. These cards represent concepts like balance, duality, and even partnership. These concepts can also be seen in some of the major arcana cards, such as the emperor and empress, the lovers, and the chariot's two sphinxes. Sometimes, the two cards will represent a choice that you have to make between two opposing or mutually exclusive options. Another common interpretation is the union of two opposing forces or options for the purpose of moving forward, similarly to the chariot card of the major arcana.

3 — The third step along this journey is the 3 cards. These cards represent concepts like creativity, growth, or completion. Some of these concepts can be seen within the major arcana as well, but the most common interpretation for the three cards is that they represent a particular phase of a person's life, or the pursuit of a specific goal is coming to an end. This might be manifested in the form of finishing college in order to move on to your true career or completing a large artistic project that has taken up a large amount of time. Maybe you've accomplished a specific part of an overall goal, and it is time to move on to the next. Regardless of the specific details involved, the 3 cards are representative of the completion of a particular phase.

4 — The fourth step along this journey is the 4 cards. These cards represent concepts like manifestation, stability, and structure. These concepts are an organic and natural step to come to after the third. With the example of finishing college in pursuit of a particular field of work, this is the time when you would be out of school and need to find real work in order to manifest those goals and provide structure for yourself while you do so. This stage is also very representative of the concepts of foundation and endurance. This will likely be a difficult time for you, and it might even take some time for you to adjust. However, once you do, you will be able to move on easily to the next stage of your life. It is important to continue to motivate yourself, however. Endurance will be a very large part of this step and even the ones that follow.

5 — The fifth step along this journey is represented by the 5 cards. These cards commonly represent concepts like change and instability or even conflict. Cards like death and the Tower from the major arcana can represent these concepts very well. In terms of a career path or the pursuit of a specific goal, this might manifest in the form of a difficult time in your life that could distract you from your work or even as a loss of inspiration or motivation. You might be in the process of beginning a new job, and change can be difficult to handle. Your situation could fluctuate frequently, and you will need to continue to maintain stability and conquer the challenges and the obstacles in your path.

6 — The sixth step along this journey is represented by the 6 cards. These cards commonly represent concepts like communication and cooperation, as well as adjustment and alignment. Continuing with the example of a specific career path or personal goal, this will be the step when you need to learn how to overcome the difficulty and inconsistency that you encountered in the fifth card's step. You will need to learn how to communicate effectively with other people and understand the issues that you are facing more accurately in order to allow you to adjust and be able to consider your situation.

7 — The seventh step along this journey is represented by the 7 cards. These cards commonly represent concepts like assessment, reflection, and understanding. This will require you to look within and perform some introspection or meditation regarding your current situation in order to understand how to handle that situation as effectively as possible. You might need to reevaluate the way that you perceive your situation in order to be able to understand it.

8 — The eighth step along this journey is represented by the 8 cards of the minor arcana. These cards most commonly represent concepts, such as action, accomplishment, and mastery. These concepts are also represented well by some of the major arcana cards, like death and the tower, similar to the third step. This eighth step describes the unification of the lessons you would have learned in the previous cards' steps in order to master the skills that you need in order to enable you to handle your current situation and master it, allowing yourself to be "reborn" in a similar way to the end of a phase that is described by the third card. These cards also function as a gateway to the next portion of your journey through the minor arcana, allowing you to realize your goals and move onward.

9 — The ninth step along this journey is represented by the 9 cards of the minor arcana. These cards most commonly represent concepts like attainment or a period of transition where you are close to achieving your goals. This is the stage that leads up to your ultimate success regarding the goal that this journey refers to. During this stage, you will need to keep your goals in mind and avoid slowing down and losing your drive. You will need to remember to "follow-through" in order to reach those goals.

10 — The tenth and final step along this journey is represented by the 10 cards of the minor arcana. These cards most commonly represent concepts such as completion, endings, and progress. During this stage, you will be completing your goals and realizing your potential. You will have "completed your journey" and will be able to begin with new things.

Additionally, each of the four suits of the minor arcana also carries its own meanings. Each one represents its own aspect of life that will be incredibly important to the development of every person. The suit of cups is the first of these. This suit represents the element of water, as well as the astrological signs that are connected to that element. This suit commonly represents concepts like emotions, intuition, creativity, and relationships with people and things. The second suit is represented by pentacles or coins. This suit is connected to the element of earth and all of its astrological signs. This suit is most commonly used to represent concepts like materials, money, manifestation, and personal goals. The third suit is represented by swords; it is connected to the element of air, as well as the air's astrological signs. This suit is most commonly associated with concepts such as communication, intelligence, thoughts, and the truth. The fourth and final suit is represented by the wand or the stick. This suit is connected to the element of fire, as well as its astrological signs. This suit is most commonly associated with concepts like enthusiasm and energy, as well as inspiration and spirit. Each of the suits' numbered cards represents the journey to mastering the concepts and ideals of their suit. Once you know the four "domains" of each of the four suits and the linear journeys represented by their numbered cards, you will be able to understand a large majority of the tarot deck's cards much more easily.

Major Arcana

The numbers of the cards in the major arcana are also significant. These cards and their numbers were discussed in the first chapter of this book but will be recapped here in a more simplistic manner for the purpose of understanding the significance of their numbers on a deeper level.

Of course, the Fool card is the "first" of the major arcana's cards, given the number 0 to represent his potential and position as the "avatar" of the recipient along their own "fool's journey." The final card is numbered 21 and is called "the world." This card represents the unification of the concepts and the various steps of the major arcana, which will allow the "fool" or the recipient to become a "whole" person again, mentally and emotionally healthy. Each of the cards between these two, from 1 to 20, has its own numerological associations, which you can apply to gain a better understanding of where it stands along the fool's journey.

The major arcana cards go above the 10-card structure of the minor arcana's numbered cards but can still be applied to those steps even beyond the number 10 at a basic level. For example, the tower card is labeled with the number 16, as the 16th step in the fool's journey. The numbers 1 and 6 can be added together to create a sum of 7, which is about assessment and evaluation. These are very important parts of the tower's emphasis on change and new beginnings. This is not the most comprehensive explanation of the tower card but can still serve to help in explaining the tower card or whichever card you might want to understand better. However, double-digit numerology will be much more effective and helpful in allowing you to understand the meanings of the major arcana cards and their numbers. A great example of this concept would be the death card, which is labeled with the number 13. The number 13 is typically considered an "unlucky" or "evil" number because of its connection to concepts like death or karmic debt. These associations will be very important in understanding the death card.

Master Numbers in Numerology

Another interesting concept that is very important to the major arcana is the "master number." This is another term that comes from numerology. There are three different "master numbers," which are 11, 22, and 33. Some sources might include 44, 55, and 66 as additional master numbers, but this is false. Not just any number with repeating twinned digits is a master number; the master numbers are specific to the numbers 1, 2, and 3 because of the "triangle of enlightenment" that they form. The master numbers are connected to numerology and numerological life paths, as well. Other numbers like the master numbers that are made from a pair of the same digit are referred to as power numbers in the field of numerology; however, this section will be focusing on only the master numbers.

The first master number is 11. This is the most intuitive of the master numbers, and it represents a connection with the unconscious mind. The 11 represents concepts like insight, emotional and mental sensitivity, and intuition. The number 11 is charged with charismatic energy and the ability to lead and inspire other people. It also represents duality in all of its positive and negative aspects, which can manifest as harmony or as discord and conflict. The potential of this number is largely dependent on the amount of direction that it has and the amount of focus that it is given toward its goals. Much like the magician or justice, the 11 walks a thin line between greatness and self-destruction at all times, and it will need to balance dreams with discipline.

The second master number is called the master builder, which has the potential to be the most successful of the master numbers. The 22 has the ability to transform dreams into reality, both of its own and others, when it is supported by the other numbers around it. The number 22 is similar to 11 but differs in its focus on practicality and logic. It faces an opposite problem to the 11 in the sense that it can lean too heavily on logic and reasoning and needs to pair them with dreams, goals, and ambition in order to reach its full potential.

The third master number is 33. This number is often referred to as the master teacher and is the most spiritually inclined of the three master numbers. The number 33 is the most influential of all numbers; it combines the numbers 11 and 22, boosting their potential to another level. It is also important to note, however, that the weakness of 33 is its inability to reach its potential on its own. Instead of taking its own action, 33 devotes itself to lifting up those around it with an extremely high level of devotion.

These three numbers relate to numerology and life paths, which are calculated by adding up the separate digits of the day that you were born on. For example, if your birthday was on February second of 1980, then you would add the month, day, and the four digits from the year. These numbers would be 2, 2, 1, 9, 8, and 0 and would add up to 22, which would align you with the master number 22. Most of the time, numbers with multiple digits are added together to get a single-digit value, but the master numbers stay how they are. If you were born on December 25, 1995, then you would need to add together 1 and 2 for the month, 2 and 5 for the day, and 1, 9, 9, and 5 for the year to get 34 which you would then add together to get 7.

Of course, these master numbers and other concepts from numerology also relate to the tarot. The single-digit numbers and 10 each have their own meanings within numerology and connect to the tarot's minor arcana, and the master numbers can be connected to the major arcana. The master builder, 22, is more directly associated with the major arcana than the other two. The major arcana has 22 cards in total, possibly because of the nature of the number's significance and its potential, which mirror the fool's potential as he completes his journey through the major arcana's numbered cards.

The number 22 can be associated by either the fool or the world, as both can be considered the "last" or 22nd card in the major arcana, which is fitting for the number and the duality and potential that it represents so strongly. The fool represents the dangers of acting carelessly and the importance of understanding your potential in order to grow and become "whole," while the world represents the realization of your potential and the act of achieving your goals. These two seemingly opposite cards are very fitting for the master-builder number, as they represent the seemingly unlimited potential that this number carries while also highlighting the dangers of acting carelessly and without direction in the same way that the fool does before he begins his journey in the narrative of the major arcana's fool's journey. The fool needs to open his eyes to the world around him and have a clear path, or he will risk stepping carelessly and obliviously off a cliff.

Chapter 6: Tarot and the Zodiac

Numerology is not the only study that tarot cards are connected to. Each of the cards and the different suits is associated with one of the four classical elements and the three astrological signs that are represented by that element. Once you are able to understand and remember which elements and which astrological signs are connected to each of the suits and individual cards in your tarot deck, you will have a much easier time understanding the meanings of each of the cards in that deck and be able to perform readings much more easily than you would otherwise be able to do. This chapter will be discussing these associations between the tarot and astrology.

The Suits and Their Corresponding Signs

The first suit that will be discussed here is the suit of cups. The cups represent the element of water, which comes from the cup's own connection to the water in a number of different religions and practices. Cups are literally used to hold liquids and can act as a vessel for the water that is represented by this suit. Modern playing card decks often replace the suit of cups with a symbol that represents a heart. This is because the cups are most commonly associated with concepts like feelings and emotions, as well as love, romance, and other kinds of relationships with other people or objects. This can be thought of as similar to the way that the cup is connected to the water it holds. The flexibility and fluidity of water are also important, as the water is able to adapt to its environment, being calm or active to fit its surroundings. The astrological signs that are represented by the element of water and its tarot suit of cups are Cancer, Pisces, and Scorpio.

The second suit is called the coins or sometimes, pentacles. The coins represent the element of earth, which comes from the coin's literal connection to the earth, having originally come from the earth itself, as well as "earthly desires" such as money or wealth, personal goals, and manifestation, as well as the body. In modern playing card decks, the suit of coins or pentacles has been replaced with diamonds, which represent the same or similar concepts to the original coin suit. The suit of coins can be thought of as a simple representation of our desires and goals, as modern life is largely fueled by financial goals and desires, or in the form of the pentacles that can represent our nature as beings that came from the earth and are supported by it. The astrological signs that are represented by the element of earth and the suit of coins or pentacles are Capricorn, Taurus, and Virgo.

The third suit that will be discussed here is called the swords. This suit is often considered to be the most logical of the four suits, having a connection to concepts, such as intelligence, as well as ideas, thoughts, and order and the communication that is required in order to convey those thoughts and concepts and the truth. In most modern playing card decks, the sword is replaced by a symbol representing a spade. The suit of swords can be thought of as a simple representation of the logic and thoughts that are required of a successful swordsman. This suit is represented by the astrological signs of Gemini, Libra, and Aquarius.

The fourth and last suit of the tarot's minor arcana is the wands. This suit was originally referred to as the sticks but was changed to wands in order to more accurately embody the element of fire. Similarly to the more mundane objects that are used to represent the other elements and their suits, the element of fire is perceived as much more mystical than the other three elements. Fire has allowed humankind to develop much further than they were able to before its discovery as a tool that we have access to. It allowed us to create machines and shape the world, and it is arguably one of the most versatile tools that humans have at their disposal while simultaneously damaging us if we come too close to it, burning our skin. As a result, we have to maintain a safe distance and take care when working with this element. Additionally, the other three classical elements all exist on their own as physical objects. The water and earth exist on their own, and the air exists as all of the particles that rise and are captured within the sky. Fire stands out as a unique case as it is not a physical object. This element exists as a force, being made up of excited particles filled with energy. The wand is similar, in the sense that it represents a much more mystical and uncommon object that the other three suits. The suit of wands, in more modern playing card decks, has been replaced by a number of different symbols like clubs, clovers, flowers, sticks or batons, and the cross. The suit of wands can be seen as a representation of our connection to magic or to the divine, as the wand or cross would suggest, and to forces like the element of fire, which we might not completely understand yet, but which can help us to grow and develop once we are able to form a stronger understanding of them. The astrological signs that the suit of wands is connected to are the three fire signs, which are Aries, Leo, and Sagittarius.

Court Cards

In addition to each of the suits, the court cards of each suit also have an element that it is associated with, meaning each of the court cards can be used to represent two different elements, with one from its suit and one from its title. The suit's element represents the forces and concepts that the card works in, while the court card's role represents the approach or the method that each court card takes in their actions and in dealing with its suit element. For example, queens are represented by water and are usually gifted with wisdom or inner knowledge and empathy for other people or things. The queen of coins, which is the suit representative of the earth, would be helpful and generous to others in their financial or otherwise personal goals and will usually have a great amount of wisdom to share with those around her.

The page is the first and the least experienced of the court cards. Pages represent the element of earth, and they embody curiosity, more than anything else. They are eager to learn and willing to explore all of the possibilities that their suit presents. This represents eagerness, almost bordering on greed, for the different opportunities that they will find in their suit. They also crave representations of the suit that they belong to, especially physical ones that can be held or felt in some way. For the Page of air, they might want to learn or study the theory of certain disciplines.

The knight is the second court card, one rank up from the page. Knights are representative of the element of fire, and they embody concepts like passion or energy. The knights are eager for action, always trying to find something that will keep them busy in some way or another. The knight would be very eager to prove themselves, and it might even need to keep that eagerness in check, or they might risk falling out of control. This can sometimes manifest as impatience. The knight of air might throw themselves wholeheartedly into their studies, always looking for some new area of study to branch into or might focus on one area relentlessly. The knight of earth, on the other hand, might throw themselves into their work in a similar way, always looking for something to do and excelling in their work, often going above and beyond even when they do not necessarily need to. These are the people who will become masters in their field of study or work or expert strategists, provided that they are able to reign in their eagerness and focus on finding direction, applying their skills toward a specific goal, as opposed to constantly looking for new skills to master.

The queen is the third court card, only one rank lower than the king. The queen is also considered the counterpart to the king, both in title and function. She represents the element of water and embodies the pursuit of knowledge that comes from within, as opposed to learning new skills based on the world around them, like the knight and page. The queen is a source of wisdom, seeking to grow her inner knowledge. She is quieter than the court members below her and much more reserved. She focuses on inspiring and helping others through their pursuit of her own self-improvement. The queen or air or earth, for example, might excel in her work through her pursuit of excellence, but her own skills are not the area in which she shines. The queen would serve as a source of inspiration, possibly even to the knight or page. Her quiet, disciplined brand of enthusiasm for her craft would serve to inspire the people who witness it, motivating them to develop their own skills in her footsteps. The queen, while likely more capable than her peers, chooses to adopt a leadership role in order to elevate the potential of the people around her or in her "court."

The fourth, final, and highest-ranking court card is the king. The king is considered to be the embodiment of their suit and the element that it is associated with. The king represents the element of air, and as such, he is level-headed and intellectual, approaching their goals with ambition and drive. The king would need to be able to think strategically and have clear goals, as well as the ability to communicate those goals effectively to other people. The king is a leader, much like the queen, but leads using their own excellence to guide others instead of motivating them to take their own action.

Cardinal, Fixed, and Mutable Signs

While these sets of associations between the suits and court cards to their respective elements and astrological signs are very helpful methods of dissecting and understanding the different cards and their meanings, there is also another approach that can be helpful. If you've ever looked into your zodiac sign or astrology, then you might have noticed a label of "cardinal, fixed, or mutable" on each sign. These labels are connected to the tarot as well. The cardinal signs are representative of the queen; the fixed signs represent the knight, and the mutable signs represent the kings.

The cardinal signs, or the signs aligned with the queens, are considered to be more assertive and aggressive. They take their own action and act in order to motivate others and allow others to shine with the element that they are associated with. Each of the signs represents the earliest stage of their season, as well. Aries is the cardinal fire sign, associated with the beginning of the spring. Cancer is the cardinal water sign, commonly associated with the beginning of the summer. Libra is the cardinal air sign, associated with the beginning of the fall. Capricorn is the cardinal earth sign, associated with the beginning of the winter season.

The fixed signs, or the signs aligned with the knights, are considered to be more focused and driven. The fixed signs are reliable and determined, sometimes even to the point of stubbornness. Each of these signs represents the height of their season. Taurus is the fixed earth sign associated with the spring. Leo is the fixed fire sign, commonly associated with the summer. Scorpio is the fixed water sign, associated with the fall. Aquarius is the fixed air sign, associated with the winter season.

The mutable signs, the signs aligned with the kings, are considered to be more adaptable and flexible. The kings are excellent communicators and can sometimes even be rebellious or difficult to deal with. Each of these signs represents the final portion of their season. The Gemini is the mutable air sign, associated with the end of the spring season. Virgo is the mutable earth sign, commonly associated with the end of the summer season. Sagittarius is the mutable fire sign, associated with the end of the fall season. Pisces is the mutable water sign, associated with the end of the winter season. The page is not assigned to any of the astrological signs, as the ranks of each of the signs and their roles come from a tradition that excludes the page from this list. The reason for this is that the page is still "undeveloped," and has the potential to move on to any of the three court titles.

Chapter 7: Tarot and the Chakras

Another very useful thing that you can learn in order to help you understand the tarot a little better is the concept of chakras, as well as how those chakras work and how they relate to the tarot. The chakras, in simple terms, are the seven "centers" of energy within the human body, and most people choose to visualize the chakras as "wheels" of energy that exist within the body, roughly along the spine. There are seven chakras within the human body, existing in a more spiritual or metaphysical sense rather than literally being organs within the body. However, the chakras can be thought of as similar to the organs in the sense that while our physical organs keep our physical bodies running and ideally in good shape, the chakras serve the same purpose for a person's soul and allow it to continue to be healthy if they are maintained and able to function properly. These chakras serve different purposes that all relate to the emotional aspect and well-being of a person. In order for a person to live a happy and successful life, it is important for them to maintain their chakras, in the same way that a physically healthy person will take care of their body.

The Importance of Balance of the Chakras

Most people experience some sort of disturbance or imbalance in their chakras at some point throughout their life. You might wake up one morning and feel a little off-center or unusual, somehow different from how you normally feel, but you just can't place it. It is more than likely that this disturbance was caused by an imbalance in your chakras and will possibly be solved with a little care of those chakras. This can be helpful in one's day-to-day life to help you to be "at your best" and understand and handle your problems much more confidently. Most commonly, these problems are caused by significant events or changes in a person's life that they are unable to handle mentally and emotionally at the time that the event occurs. You might have had a serious physical illness and be forced to focus on physical or financial recovery or some sort of emotional disturbance, like the end of a significant long-term relationship. In these cases, it can be incredibly helpful for you to understand which chakras relate to these different aspects of yourself in order to deal with them as effectively as you can and continue to be healthy and happy. You could even choose to perform daily "maintenance" for your chakras in order to keep your emotional, mental, and spiritual health in good shape. In some cases, they can also help your physical body to function more smoothly since the body and spirit are connected and part of every person.

There are a number of methods that you can use in order to realign your chakras and get them to work properly or simply to keep them that way, thereby avoiding a lot of potential unnecessary imbalance within you. One of these methods is meditation. Meditation is a helpful tool that can help you to understand a lot of different issues that you might experience, and this applies just as well to spiritual matters. Another method, of course, is by using divination to help you to understand your issues and how to resolve them. This chapter will be about the use of the tarot cards and divinatory tarot readings for the purpose of aligning your chakras and keeping your spirit healthy.

There are different kinds of divination tools that can help you with this, but the practice of tarot reading is one of the most effective tools. For one, it can help you pin down the specific problem that you might be facing if you do not already understand it, as well as the areas that need attention because of that issue. Tarot is a much more direct and specific kind of tool for divination in a very detailed way, especially when compared to other kinds of divinatory methods because of the nature of how tarot cards reveal information about the reader or the recipient of the reading.

When you are performing a tarot reading for this purpose, you will want to start out by shuffling your tarot deck. Think about the different chakras as you do and the states that they are in, as well as why this might be the case. You should have a specific question in mind, performing the reading to help you to understand that question. Your seven chakras and their health would be a great topic to focus on to help you to understand each of the chakras within your body. Once your deck has been shuffled, you will need to draw seven cards from your deck, drawing one card for each chakra. You will also need to remember the order you drew these cards, so it will be important to remember that when you draw and lay your cards on the table. Additionally, there are different ways that different people will use to draw their cards. Some people will simply pull from the top of their deck, while some people might split or cut their deck and draw their cards from one or both halves of the deck, some people will fan their decks out and choose the cards that speak out to them, and some people might even choose to simply go down the stack and pull cards out either at random or with a specific system that speaks to them. It is important that when you are drawing your cards, you use whatever method feels "right" to you and pull out the cards that you feel are the "correct" cards for yourself. Choose your seven cards and lay your spread. For a reading regarding your chakras, you will want to lay your cards out in the same arrangement as your seven chakras, which is in a vertical line. The first card that you draw will go at the bottom, representing your root chakra, and the seventh card that you draw will go to the top to represent your crown chakra. The cards should not make contact with any of the other cards but spaced out separately. The reasoning for this is simply to allow you to remember which card corresponds to the chakras more easily, but it is also meant to represent the separate locations of the chakras along your spine and your perception of them and the situation that you find yourself in.

Your cards should be on your table, or a similar flat surface, facing downward so that you cannot read them yet at this point, but they should be arranged in such a way that you can flip them and read them when you are ready. But before you do so, you should try to stop for a moment and consider the cards that lay in front of you. Take a moment to think about what you feel before you read the cards in front of you. What are your thoughts regarding those seven cards? You should be listening to your "gut" or your intuition for the answer, as well as any significant signs that your body might be sending to you or any messages that might be coming from your unconscious mind. You might begin to feel pressure in a certain part of your body or some other form of discomfort or anxiety. These kinds of signals can serve to help you to understand the state of your chakras on a deeper level before you begin your reading. You might even notice that a specific card or multiple cards might seem different from the others. They might be shifted in slightly different positions from the rest of your cards, and you might even literally begin to see certain cards as darker or "blurred," making it harder for you to focus on that card or cards. These can be signs that those chakras are blocked and need to be cleared, or you might need to take more care of those chakras in comparison to the others. On the other hand, "brighter" cards or the ones that you find you can focus on much more clearly will act as signs that those chakras are functioning especially well, or at least better than some of the others. Intuition can be a very useful tool, and it can be important to reach out to your intuition and your unconscious mind for guidance from time to time. Taking a moment to actively reach out to them before a tarot reading can prime you for that tendency and strengthen your connection to those parts of yourself and even to the chakras that you are focusing on. You might even find that you have already answered your initial question to some degree. Do not stop there, though. You should still continue on with the reading, looking to the cards to confirm any suspicions that you might have or pointing you in the correct direction if those suspicions are not completely true.

Why You Need to Read Your Tarot Cards

The last thing that you will need to do during this reading, of course, is to read your cards. At this step in the process, you will need to understand the meanings of the cards within the tarot deck. The various cards and the meanings of those cards are discussed in this book, and information on those cards can be found in the first chapter for the major arcana, the fourth and fifth chapters for the minor arcana (the numbered cards in the fourth chapter and the court cards in the fifth chapter), and the history and theory of the tarot in the second and third chapters. Additionally, most tarot decks will also include a short book about the different cards and how to read them; you can use this to help you interpret the reading. However, chakra readings are usually much easier than most other spreads, because the cards that you have drawn and laid out already have a specific meaning and relate to a specific question almost inherently.

Each card will be read with regards to the specific chakra that it represents in the order that you have laid them out on the surface. You will want to be looking for specific information about the chakra that the card relates to. Each of the seven chakras has its own rules and relates to its own areas of your life and your well-being. Each chakra can also be blocked by specific kinds of events that might happen throughout your life or experiences that you might be having at the moment. Additionally, you will need to understand the seven chakras, as well as the different kinds of experiences or circumstances that can block them. Read on to know more about the chakras and the ways that they work.

The Chakras and the Tarot

As mentioned earlier, the seven chakras are arranged along the spine, starting from the base going to the top of the head or the crown. The first one is at the base of the spine and is called the root chakra. The root chakra is the first you will need to draw and read a card for. The root chakra affects all of your basic survival functions and needs. The card that you drew for this chakra will let you know about the condition of this chakra and if its basic needs are being met. If it is in good shape, then you are healthy, at least with regards to your root chakra and the parts of yourself that it governs. If it is in a particularly poor condition, then it is likely that this chakra is blocked, and its basic needs are not being met. This will typically require some level of "chakra work," usually in the form of meditation. The root chakra is very commonly associated with the red color, and focusing on this color and the needs or the root chakra while you meditate on that chakra can be helpful in healing or "unblocking" it.

The second card that you will be reading is also for the second chakra, which is referred to as the "sacral" chakra. This is above the root chakra and is located below the navel, usually about three inches down at the center of the lower belly. The sacral chakra is associated with physical feelings and sensations and is commonly related to your sexuality and sex organs. If this chakra is blocked, the cause is usually guilt or a similar negative emotion. Other common causes of a blocked sacral chakra are loneliness or feelings of neglect. Regular meditation on the sacral chakra can help clear it out if it becomes blocked, and other things like adopting healthier lifestyles and physical activity can also help to clear out blockages in your sacral chakra. Focusing on color orange while meditating on this chakra can also help clear it out more effectively.

The third card that you will be reading is for the "solar plexus" chakra, which is located on the upper belly, around where the diaphragm rests or near the sternum. The solar plexus chakra is associated with things like willpower and confidence. This chakra is what causes that "chest puff" when you are proud of something you have accomplished or what causes your heart to feel empty or cold when you are scared or sad. If this chakra is blocked, the reason is usually something similar to shame or a lack of accomplishment. Regular meditation on the solar plexus chakra can help clear it out if it becomes blocked or is underperforming. Other things like "getting a win," accomplishing goals, following through a task, or performing a job that you are proud of can help improve the flow of energy in the solar plexus chakra. Focusing on the yellow color while meditating on this chakra can also help clear it out more effectively.

The fourth card that you will be reading is for the "heart" chakra. This is located in the middle of the chest, above the solar plexus. The heart chakra is associated with things like love, compassion, and relationships with other people. This is where you will feel, most heavily, the weight of a wrong that has been committed against you. You can also notice this weight when you forgive someone or accept a situation that you have been struggling with, especially for a long time. If this chakra is blocked, the cause is usually something similar to a grudge that you might be holding or another kind of unresolved trauma or experience that affected you deeply. Regular meditation on the heart chakra can help clear it out if it becomes blocked. Other ways to improve the state of your heart chakra are giving forgiveness or letting go of your unresolved issues. Focusing on the color green while you meditate on this chakra can also help clear it out better.

The fifth card that you will be reading is for the "throat" chakra. This is located in the middle of the neck or throat, and it is associated with things like your ability to "speak out" and general communication, including your voice. If this chakra is blocked, it could mean that you are not receiving the whole truth, or you are haunted by the feeling of guilt for lying to or deceiving someone else. Regular meditation on the throat chakra can help clear its negative energy. Things, like being more honest and open and trying to encourage openness and honesty in others, can effectively unblock this chakra. Remember that open communication is the cure to a blocked throat chakra. Focusing on the color blue while you meditate on this chakra can also help clear it out.

The sixth card that you will be reading is for the "third eye" chakra. This is located between the eyes on your forehead, where the third eye is believed to exist. The third eye chakra is associated with things like the "sixth sense" or things that you might not be able to physically see with your "real eyes." This sixth sense is based on intuition and insight, similar to the concept of the personal unconscious, and it shapes the way that you perceive certain things that have a strong impact on you. Some people are especially more sensitive or aware of their "sixth sense" or their personal unconscious and might experience a blockage of this chakra in the form of a headache. Regular meditation on the third eye chakra can help clear it out if it becomes blocked or inactive. Focusing on the color indigo while you meditate on this chakra can also help clear it out better.

The seventh and last card that you will be reading is for the "crown" chakra. This is located at the top of your head or the crown. This is also the "last" chakra on the list. The crown chakra is associated with things like your connection to the divine or the universe, depending on your religious practice or belief. A healthy crown chakra represents a healthy connection to your deity or deities or a strong sense of faith in the general sense if you do not worship a deity. If this chakra is blocked, the cause is usually something similar to "spiritual greed," or focusing more on yourself rather than on what you put out into the world. Regular meditation on the crown chakra can help clear it out if it becomes blocked. Also, strengthening your connection to your faith or the divine will improve the energy surrounding this chakra. Focusing on the colors of violet or white while you meditate on this chakra can also help clear the negative energy affecting the crown.

Chapter 8: Tarot and Religion

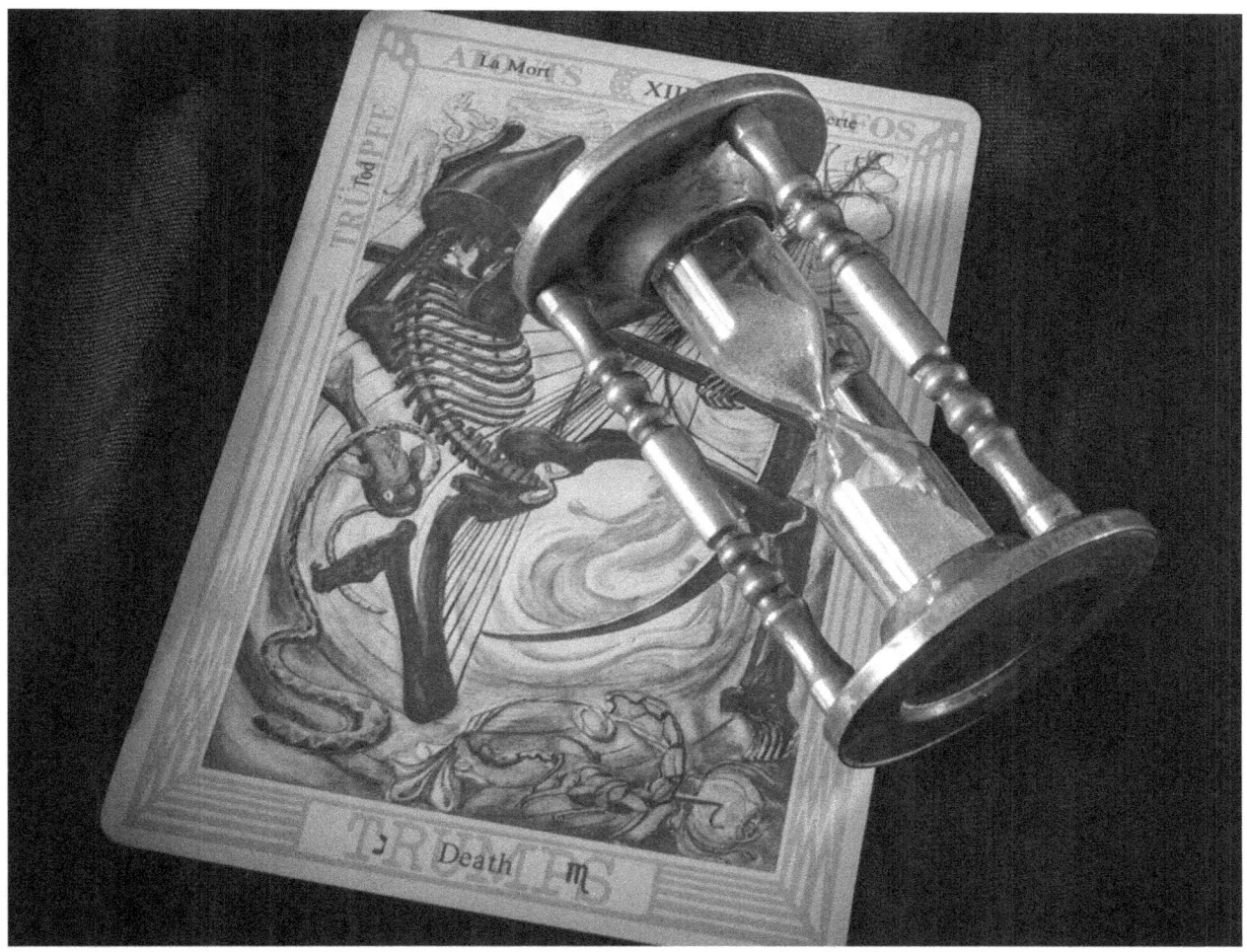

Another important thing to consider with regards to tarot and the use of tarot cards for divinatory purposes is religion. A big question that might come up when considering its use to perform divination is: "Is this okay with my religion?" This is, of course, a very important point to consider, especially for people who are devoted to their religion and religious practices. Christianity is likely one of the most significant religions to consider since it is one of the most popular religions practiced in the world and one that has the strongest prejudice against practices like divination. Many Christians will cite Bible verses or other similar sources with regards to these kinds of "occult" practices like divination, claiming that they are sinful, even satanic in nature. Some of the most common Bible verses that are used to condemn the use of practices like these are as follows:

Here is Leviticus 19:31, which is stated in the King James Version:
"Regard not them that have familiar spirits, neither seek after wizards, to be defiled by them: I [am] the LORD your God."

Here is Leviticus 20:27, also from the King James Version:
"A man also or woman that hath a familiar spirit, or that is a wizard, shall surely be put to death: they shall stone them with stones: their blood [shall be] upon them."

Deuteronomy 18:10, 18:11, and 18:12, from the King James Version:
"There shall not be found among you [any one] that maketh his son or his daughter to pass through the fire, [or] that useth divination, [or] an observer of times, or an enchanter, or a witch. Or a charmer, or a consulter with familiar spirits, or a wizard, or a necromancer. For all that do these things [are] an abomination unto the LORD: and because of these abominations, the LORD thy God doth drive them out from before thee."

Jeremiah 27:9 and 27:10, from the King James Version:
"Therefore, hearken not ye to your prophets, nor to your diviners, nor to your dreamers, nor to your enchanters, nor to your sorcerers, which speak unto you, saying, Ye shall not serve the king of Babylon: For they prophesy a lie unto you, to remove you far from your land; and that I should drive you out, and ye should perish."

As you can see, these verses essentially state that faithful Christians should not allow themselves to be persuaded by "those with familiar spirits" or "wizards," which, in this context, refers to those who practice witchcraft, divination, or other magical traditions, specifically ones that require the user to act in ways that go against the word of the Lord. They also condemn the use of prophecy from sources other than the Lord or agents of the Lord, as well as divination or enchanters. It would seem, at a surface level, that the word of the Bible and the Lord, by extension, would condemn the use of divinatory practices, like the tarot readings that are described in this book. However, the divination that is referred to in the Bible, while it wears the same name, is not the same kind of "divination" that is performed in tarot readings at all. Yes, the Bible does literally use the word divination, as do tarot readings, but only for lack of a more accurate term for the practice. The kind of divination referred to in these verses is specific to magical divination that relies on the use of "familiar spirits," which essentially means that in order for these "rules" or "laws" to apply based on "the spirit of the law," the divinatory practices in question would need to be the sort that relies on "familiar spirits" from religions that defy the word of the Christian God or the Lord, such as those who devoutly practiced religions that were being encountered for the first time or had recently been encountered for the first time when the Bible was recorded.

The practice of performing divinatory tarot readings absolutely does not apply to any of these verses, nor do they apply to similar verses condemning the use of magic, witchcraft, or any other sort of unholy practices unless the cards themselves are made from materials that should not be combined according to the word of the Bible. As has been mentioned in this book, the use of tarot cards for divinatory purposes relies more heavily on psychology rather than unexplained magic, and unless a version of the Bible is released that condemns the use of tarot cards specifically or the use of psychology, then any Christian person should be relatively "safe." It is, however, important to consider these verses (if you are a Christian) and any other sources that might be relevant to your own religion, as it is always better to be safe than sorry.

Indeed, it is worth considering what your specific religion has to say about this practice as your religion may frown upon the Tarot, or even outright ban it. If you have any specific questions, it would be wise to consult with your religious leaders so that they may be to give you proper guidance and counsel on what is permitted and what is not. The last thing we want to do is to give you advice that may contradict your faith. Everything here is present in good faith. As such, please take it as an exercise in the use of psychology rather than engaging in inappropriate practices.

Conclusion

Thank you very much for having taken the time to read this book. By now, we hope that you have gotten a good sense of what the Tarot is and what it can be used for. In addition, we hope that you have gained a different perspective on it. We sincerely hope that if you had ever believed it to be quackery or even a means of fooling people out of their money, you have now gained a different perception of it.

At this point, please go over any parts or chapters, which you feel you need to brush up on. In doing so, you will be able to improve your overall understanding of the subject matter. Furthermore, you will be able to interpret each of the cards based on sound fundamentals rather than apparent mystical or supernatural powers.

Additionally, do take the time to reflect on the discoveries which you have made about yourself or even human nature for that matter. We are confident that you have gained a newfound sense of understanding of the underlying motivations of the people around you. As you begin to see the archetypes we have discussed in action, you will begin to really see how and why people act the way they do. This will help you to avoid feeling confused by seemingly erratic behavior. As a matter of fact, your understanding of human nature will lead you to become far more insightful and wiser.

The fact of the matter is that by learning more about yourself and your feelings, you will not only grow spiritually but also intellectually. Consequently, you have a great deal to gain from using the Tarot to further your journey of self-discovery and personal development. We hope that this book will be able to give you just the boost you need along this path.

Thanks again for choosing this book. We feel that with the number of options out there. It can be hard to tell which sources of information are legit and which ones are just a bunch of baloney. Great care was taken in ensuring that the information in this book is forthcoming and honest. The last thing we want to do is to give you false, or otherwise misleading information about the Tarot and how it can be used to improve your outlook on life, and yourself.

If you have found this book to be useful and informative, by all means tell your friends, family, and colleagues about it. We hope that they, too, will find it to be useful and informative. If you feel compelled to share your knowledge with others who might be interested in this topic, then you can certainly use this book as a reference to guide you. We are sure that plenty of folks out there would be interested to know more about the Tarot in a truthful and honest manner. Plus, it can make a great topic of conversation at a dinner party when spending time with friends and family.

See you next time!

www.ingramcontent.com/pod-product-compliance
Lightning Source LLC
Chambersburg PA
CBHW081753100526
44592CB00015B/2407